BIRD
IDENTIFICATION
AND FIELDCRAFT

BIRD
IDENTIFICATION
AND FIELDCRAFT

A BIRDWATCHER'S GUIDE

MARK WARD

NH
NEW
HOLLAND

First published in 2005 by New Holland Publishers (UK) Ltd
London • Cape Town • Sydney • Auckland

www.newhollandpublishers.com

Garfield House, 86–88 Edgware Road, London W2 2EA, United Kingdom

80 McKenzie Street, Cape Town 8001, South Africa

14 Aquatic Drive, Frenchs Forest, NSW 2086, Australia

218 Lake Road, Northcote, Auckland, New Zealand

ISBN 1 84330 887 8

Publishing Manager: Jo Hemmings
Project Editor: Camilla MacWhannell
Cover Design and Design: Gülen Shevki-Taylor
Editor: Ben Hoare
Production: Joan Woodroffe

Reproduction by Modern Age Repro Co., Hong Kong
Printed and bound in Malaysia by Times Offset (M) Sdn Bhd

Captions for preliminary pages
Page 1: Adult Gannet in flight
Opposite: Immature male Hen Harrier in hunting mode
Page 6: Male Brambling (top left), Starling (top right), and winter scene at Slimbridge
Wildfowl & Wetlands Trust (bottom)
Page 9: Male Lesser Spotted Woodpecker bringing food to a juvenile in the nest

CONTENTS

THE WILDLIFE TRUSTS

The Wildlife Trusts, a partnership of 47 local Wildlife Trusts, is the UK's leading voluntary organisation working, since 1912, in all areas of nature conservation. We are fortunate to have the support of more than 560,000 members, including some famous household names.

The Wildlife Trusts protect wildlife for the future by managing in excess of 2,500 nature reserves, ranging from woodlands and peat bogs, to heathlands, coastal habitats and wild flower meadows. We campaign tirelessly on behalf of wildlife, including of course the multitude of bird species.

We run thousands of events, including dawn chorus walks and birdwatching activities, as well as conservation projects involving adults and children across the UK. Every year the Leicestershire and Rutland Wildlife Trust, along with the RSPB, organises the British Birdwatching Fair at Rutland Water, a testament to the growing popularity of birdwatching and conservation in general. The Wildlife Trusts work to influence industry and government and also advise landowners on creating optimum conditions for wildlife.

As numbers of formerly common bird species plummet, we are encouraging people to take action, whether through supporting conservation organisations in their work for birds, or taking simple steps such as providing food and water for garden birds.

The Wildife Trusts manage some of the most important sites in the UK for birds. Whether it is Puffins on Skomer Island, Ospreys at Loch of the Lowes in Scotland and Rutland Water, or Bitterns at Far Ings in Lincolnshire, Wildlife Trust reserves offer fantastic birdwatching opportunities.

Whether you are a novice or an experienced birdwatcher there is always more to learn that will increase the enjoyment of birdwatching. Mark Ward has written this stimulating book to help all birdwatchers to enjoy the moment of discovery in the field. Full of inspired and practical advice on how to improve your bird identification and fieldcraft techniques, he conveys the enjoyment experienced whether simply birding in the garden, or venturing farther afield in search of rarities.

The Wildlife Trusts is a registered charity (number 207238). For membership, and other details, please phone The Wildlife Trusts on 0870 0367711, or log on to www.wildlifetrusts.org

INTRODUCTION

It was the challenge of identifying birds and using the right fieldcraft to find and observe them that first encouraged me to become a birdwatcher as a child. Now, many years later as a fully fledged birder, the same challenges keep my enthusiasm and passion for watching birds just as strong today.

You don't have to be a 'good' birdwatcher to enjoy watching birds – you don't even have to be a birdwatcher at all – but you will get a lot more satisfaction from the pastime if you are skilled in the arts of identification and fieldcraft. Being able to identify tricky species such as skulking warblers and juvenile waders, and successfully locating rare, interesting or elusive birds, are among the greatest pleasures to be had as a birdwatcher. I will never forget the thrill of identifying my first Little Stint and securing my first ever views of Bittern and Lesser Spotted Woodpecker after hours of trying.

There have been great advances in bird identification in recent years and many excellent field guides are now available to help make identifying birds an easier task. The choice can be daunting, but choosing a good one is only the first step on the road to successful bird ID. *Bird Identification and Fieldcraft* is the perfect companion to your field guide, as it actually shows you how to identify birds.

The first two chapters of this book guide you through the thought processes, practicalities and pitfalls of bird identification. They take you from the basic principles to more difficult skills, such as working out a bird's age, identifying birds in flight, and learning songs and calls. Hopefully, the book will help you to become more proficient in identification so that you can identify correctly more of the birds you see.

You need to find birds to begin with, and then obtain good views if you want to be able to identify them, so in this sense, identification and fieldcraft are inextricably linked. The second part of this book describes the techniques that will enable you to find and see birds – and to see them well. I have included some subjects that would not traditionally come under the heading of fieldcraft, such as making the most of the weather and time of year and how to watch a local 'patch', because I think they are just as important in helping you to get more from your time in the field.

Bird Identification and Fieldcraft is for anyone with an interest in birds. If you are just starting out, it will provide you with the skills and information you need to become a better birdwatcher, and if you have been birding for a while, it will show you plenty of new approaches, ideas and techniques to try that may bring you even greater rewards. If you balk at the thought of identifying raptors in flight, never seem to be in the right place at the right time, find birding in woodland a chore, or want to be able to pick out rarities from among big flocks of birds, this book is for you.

Throughout the book, I have used my own experiences as much as possible, giving relevant species of bird as examples to help you visualize various points and techniques. As well as sharing my own secrets of success, I have mentioned some of the times where I haven't been quite so fortunate in my approaches to identification and fieldcraft in the hope that you won't make the same slip-ups. I hope you will find these anecdotes entertaining as well as educational! I have also included 'top tips' throughout the book: short and snappy snippets of key information that complement the main text.

Most of all, I hope that this book will make your experiences of watching birds more fulfilling, and that after reading it, you will become a more successful birdwatcher.

BELOW: *A good view of a Treecreeper is always a treat.*

IDENTIFICATION

Depending on your point of view, the challenge of bird identification can be one of the greatest pleasures or the single most frustrating aspect of birdwatching. Birds often flit into view for just a few seconds or fly past at high speed and 'real' views can be nothing like the illustration in your identification guide, showing the perfectly posed bird in glorious close up. In addition, the same species can come in a variety of plumages and males may look very different from females. Even birds that belong to different species can look remarkably similar. Then there are the birds that will always be tricky to identify, even when you do get a good view. In fact, identifying birds is often not easy at all, but that's all part of the fun!

The secretive Corncrake may only reveal its head and neck above the grass, but its repetitive 'crex crex' song is an unmistakable aid to identification.

1 IDENTIFICATION BASICS

Bird identification is both an art and a science. A natural eye for detail is a bonus, but it is possible to develop the skills, the knowledge and the experience that will enable you to become accomplished at it and, ultimately, be able to put a name to most of the birds you see.

A good approach certainly involves looking closely at the birds' plumage, but there is much more to bird identification than that. It is equally important to get a feel for their overall character and behaviour and to remember that some species are only found at certain times of year and in certain places.

You won't get it right every time, but you will feel a great sense of satisfaction each time you do.

PRACTICE MAKES PERFECT

In the end, practice always makes perfect. The more time you spend watching birds and familiarizing yourself with the behaviour and appearance of different species, the more natural – and straightforward – bird identification will become.

Field guides are great for illustrating plumage details, but it is hard to bring birds to life and capture their 'feel' – something birdwatchers refer to as 'jizz' – in a couple of pictures. This is where building up your experience of actually seeing birds for yourself becomes so valuable in improving your identification skills. Even if you have not had much practice at identifying birds or are just starting out as a birdwatcher, I bet you know a lot more than you realize. You will almost certainly be able to

ABOVE AND LEFT: *Some birds, such as the Garden Warbler (above), are distinctly lacking in striking features while others, such as the Puffin (left), have plenty and are instantly recognizable to almost everyone.*

OPPOSITE: *The tiny size, golden-yellow crown and black-and-white wing pattern of the Goldcrest – Europe's smallest bird – is a striking combination.*

top tip

Really get to know the 50 or so species you see most regularly. Don't forget to familiarize yourself with males and females, as well as young birds and the different appearances of each species through the year.

RIGHT AND BELOW: *The Song (right) and Mistle Thrush (below) are a constant source of confusion for novice birdwatchers. They look very similar at first glance, but the differences – including the latter's larger size, greyer plumage and brash behaviour – will become obvious when you have spent time watching them.*

recognize a good number of species already.

Most people can identify a Kingfisher in a split second if one decides to zip past. The slightest glimpse of a dazzling blue-and-orange bullet speeding by is enough to tell you it is a Kingfisher, but so does the fact that it is flying over water. If you have identified a Kingfisher in this way, you have already used some of the most essential principles of bird ID: registering key features and taking into account where you saw the bird and what it was doing.

Of course, some birds are much easier to identify than others. This may be because they are brightly coloured, have a distinctive shape, behave in a certain way or because

top tip

The Dunlin is the yardstick by which to compare all small waders. Try to make sure you know it extremely well, so that finding and identifying other small waders is much simpler. The Herring Gull assumes a similar role among the large gulls, the Meadow Pipit among the pipits, and the Chiffchaff among the warblers.

there simply isn't anything else they could be. Other birds, such as the Blackbird and Robin, are easy to identify because you see so many of them, perhaps on a daily basis in your own garden. You don't need to look at either of these species for very long to know what you are looking at.

More and more birds will become like Kingfishers, Blackbirds and Robins to you as you come into contact with different species on a regular basis and make the effort to try to identify them. No one suddenly turns into an identification expert overnight, but with practice, you will correctly identify more birds and get more confident about doing so.

You will also find that you can identify birds much more quickly and from less than perfect views as you get to know their key features and become accustomed to their jizz. The reason why experienced birders can name distant shearwaters hurtling over the sea or silhouetted falcons soaring in the sky is simple. Through years of practice they have built up a mental profile of that particular species, and those with which it could be confused, enabling them to come to a rapid and (usually) correct conclusion.

ABOVE: *Despite being a common sight in most areas, the Kestrel is frequently confused with rarer falcons. Familiarizing yourself with its plumage, shape and flight mode is time well spent.*

There are some birds whose identity won't leap out at you and which cause problems for even the most experienced birdwatchers. These are the birds you will have to look at much more closely to ensure you get it right. Some people choose to ignore immature gulls, warblers and other 'little brown jobs' (or LBJs for short). But remember: successfully identifying such 'problem' birds might give you the most satisfaction.

BELOW: *The Hoopoe's pink, black and white colours, bizarre crest and curved beak render it one of the few truly unmistakable birds.*

Always make an effort to identify every bird you see or at least make an educated guess, and do not be afraid to get it wrong. You may not be right sometimes, but at least you tried. In fact, you will be surprised how many times you are right.

I made plenty of glaring errors during my formative years as a birdwatcher, but I learned from these mistakes and now make every effort to ensure I don't repeat them. Remembering where you went wrong when you misidentified birds is just as important as remembering where you went right.

BELOW: *Great Tits. Getting to know the commonest members of bird families will make it easier to identify the scarcer ones that you will encounter less often.*

GETTING TO GRIPS WITH COMMON BIRDS

Building up a sound knowledge of the commonest species of birds is the best apprenticeship any birdwatcher can serve. The first birds I became familiar with were the dozen or so species that visited my garden. After a while I began to visit my local park and, eventually, more exotic locations, but my 'life list' (the list of different species I had seen) was slow to grow at first. Looking back, it is obvious that this was a good thing as I really appreciated and looked closely at every new bird I saw, mainly because it was such a rare event!

Many people that take up birdwatching are so eager to create a big list of different species they have seen that they never get to grips with the commonest birds. They may see a lot of rare birds, but if they don't know how the White-rumped Sandpiper that they have travelled 160 kilometres (100 miles) to see differs from a Dunlin, then the whole process becomes a bit fruitless.

Once you have learned the more common species, you can quickly eliminate them from the identification equation and thus save a lot of time having to look up every bird you see in your field

LEFT: *Gardens are a great place to practise your ID skills on common birds such as these Goldfinches.*

guide. The vast majority of the birds you see will be common birds, so picking out and identifying more unusual ones will be much easier. You may not be able to identify the stranger immediately, but at least you will know it is something out of the ordinary.

A friend of mine found himself confronted with an 'odd' wader at Titchwell in Norfolk one September day. He admitted to not knowing what it was, but being familiar with the common waders on the marsh that day, he knew it was something he had not seen before. Once the more experienced birders in the hide took a look for themselves, they realized he had found the reserve's first-ever Buff-breasted Sandpiper: a rare vagrant from North America!

OPPOSITE TOP: *If you can
recognize these birds as warblers,
you are already well on the way
to identifying them as Lesser
Whitethroats (juvenile above,
adult below).*

SEXUAL DIFFERENCES AND FAMILY RESEMBLANCES

There is a considerable difference in the plumage of males and
females of some species. In fact, you could easily be fooled into
thinking you are looking at two entirely different species when
you see the males and females of many ducks and passerines
(small perching birds) side by side. In most cases, males are
brighter and more elaborately marked. This is only fair – they do
have to do the impressing when it comes to courtship! There can
also be a size difference (see page 26).

On the positive side, different families of birds share certain
characteristics. Getting to know these key features will be time
well spent. Being able to tell a tern from a gull and a thrush from
a chat is a skill that is just as important as being able to identify
individual species, so try to get to grips with the major groups. If
you have a good idea of which type of bird you are looking at,
you can concentrate your efforts on the relevant section of your
field guide instead of having to flick
through 300 pages of illustrations
hoping to chance upon the one that
matches your mystery bird.

OPPOSITE BOTTOM:
*Ducks and geese are
closely related, but when
shown alongside a
European White-fronted
Goose (above), the more
compact structure
and smaller size of the
drake Wigeon (below)
can be appreciated.*

ABOVE: *The black-and-white
male Pied Flycatcher (left) is a
much more distinctive bird than
the female (right).*

LOOKING CLOSELY

Few birds can be identified conclusively on one or two features alone, so the more you can observe, the easier it will be to identify the bird and the more certain you can be of the ID. The missing feature could turn out to be the all-important one.

Take the following imaginary description taken from a birdwatcher's notebook: 'a small bird flying around over the lake. It was black above and white below, with pointed wings and an obvious square white rump.' This sounds like a fairly comprehensive description and you may think that enough detail has been provided to identify the mystery bird. It certainly sounds like a House Martin, but due to the observer's failure to note the bird's long bill, the correct identification of Green Sandpiper (which also has all of the features given) is unlikely to be reached.

RIGHT: *The Chiffchaff: perhaps the ultimate little brown job!*

RIGHT: *The Chiffchaff: perhaps the ultimate little brown job!*

BELOW: *Divers are notoriously difficult to identify in non-breeding plumage. The Red-throated Diver can be identified from its pale grey plumage, the large amount of white on its head and neck, and the tilted position in which it holds it head and bill.*

For some families of birds, including 'grey' geese and gulls, the colour of the bare parts (the legs, feet and bill) are important to separate similar species, but for most other families, this is not really that helpful. For groups such as warblers, the presence or absence of wing-bars, a supercilium and an eyestripe are the secret to identification. Some very similar – and tricky – species can only be separated by the pattern of their tertial feathers!

The ability to look really closely at birds is invaluable. Scrutinize the entire bird and build up a picture of how it looks, from the size and shape of its bill to the pattern on the tip of its tail. Some features will be of more value than others and some may be of little use at all, but it is better to make sure you have seen and taken note of everything. Over time, you will learn which features are best for certain groups of birds and instinctively will home in on the vital parts that hold the keys to successful identification.

top tip

Get a friend to help you practise your identification skills. If they cover up the captions next to the illustrations in bird books and test you on the pictures, you can practise identifying birds on the occasions when you can't get into the field.

BIRD BITS

I have been baffled on more than one occasion by people asking me to identify a bird they have seen with a 'black head', only to find the bird in question is a male Blackcap, which actually has a grey head with a black cap. It's only words, but you see my point.

ABOVE: *Juvenile waders always present an identification challenge. The pale plumage, long, upturned bill and 'elegant' proportions of this one should tell you it is a Greenshank. Its green legs are a bit of a giveaway, too!*

CROWN
FOREHEAD
EAR-COVERTS
BILL
NAPE
THROAT
BREAST
MANTLE
LESSER COVERTS
MEDIAN COVERTS
SCAPULARS
BACK
GREATER COVERTS
TERTIALS
ALULA
RUMP
FLANK
UPPER TAIL-COVERTS
BELLY
VENT
SECONDARIES
PRIMARIES
PRIMARY COVERTS
TAIL
UNDER TAIL-COVERTS

There is no need to be an expert on what is referred to as bird topography – the different parts of a bird – but knowing the major bird 'bits' can be very useful. Start by learning the correct names for just a few parts and progress from there.

Believe me, it can really help to use phrases such as 'dark grey mantle', 'pale primary tips' and 'red orbital ring' when you are describing a bird to other birdwatchers. Such precise descriptions enable them to visualize the bird accurately. Of course, it also makes you look ever so knowledgeable!

From an identification point of view, it also encourages you to look a bit closer at the parts of a bird and to see how the feathers all fit together. Being able to locate and home in on the primary coverts of a bird is not an urgent requirement, but do try to get to grips with the main areas.

ABOVE: *Little Owls are often seen at dusk when their plumage details can be hard to see. Their dumpy shape, hunched posture and Blackbird size give them an unmistakable jizz, though.*

SIZE AND SHAPE

Many birds have distinctive shapes and this, together with the size of the bird you are looking at, can be as crucial as plumage when it comes to identification.

Glaucous and Iceland Gulls are virtually identical in plumage at all ages, but are very different in size and structure. The former is about the same size as a Great Black-backed Gull, and is rather 'mean-looking', with a square head and huge beak. The latter is more like a Herring Gull in size, proportionately longer-winged, and has a 'gentler' expression due to its round head and small bill. All of which gives these

BELOW: *The Eider's 'ski-slope' head and bill give it a distinctive profile. This is a particularly useful feature for identifying the brown female (top).*

similarly plumaged species a totally different shape and jizz.

With waders, leg length and the length and shape of the bill can also be useful, especially if you have several species side by side for direct comparison. Fortunately, you will often enjoy this luxury, as waders are sociable birds that mix freely.

Be careful when assessing size and shape, because the way birds stand or sit can exaggerate or hide their true form. They stretch up their necks and puff out their bodies when alarmed, so they can appear a lot bigger than they really are and can change shape in the blink of an eye! They also fluff up their feathers in cold weather, and may look sleek and slender after bathing.

The size of high-flying birds can be particularly difficult to assess, and looking through optics will always give you a false impression of size. Even flying insects can momentarily

ABOVE: *The Bewick's Swan (left) has more black than yellow on its bill, but its smaller size and goose-like structure are just as useful when it comes to separating it from the Whooper Swan (right).*

BELOW: *The Little Grebe has a 'powder puff' rear end, giving it the roundest and most compact shape of all the grebes.*

top tip

Size comparisons are always helpful, so look around for natural features and other birds nearby that might give you a clue to a bird's size. Size (and shape) comparisons with a species you know well may also be useful pointers to the identity of your mystery bird.

masquerade as birds when they become magnified in your binoculars while you are scanning into the distance.

There can also be considerable variation in size within species. Just because two birds are different sizes, it does not mean they are different species. Most birds show a slight difference in size between sexes, but for some, the difference can be striking. The female Ruff is much smaller than the male, for example.

Many birdwatchers decide they have seen a rare Goshawk when they encounter a female Sparrowhawk because it is so much larger than the male (a common trait among raptors, known as sexual size dimorphism). These two closely related species – a frequent source of confusion for beginners – provide a good example of the relative merits of structural differences and plumage for separating similar species and demonstrate that size can be misleading.

ABOVE: A slender, 'Swift-shaped' falcon hunting persistently and expertly for dragonflies will almost certainly be a Hobby.

BELOW: The Nuthatch can climb headfirst down tree trunks as well as up: a unique feat.

LOOKS AREN'T EVERYTHING

What is it doing?

If you see a long-billed, long-legged bird wandering around on the beach, probing its beak into the mud, it will almost certainly be a wader. If you see a small brown bird creeping up the side of a tree, then there is a good chance it will be a Treecreeper. It's a simple concept, but thinking about how a bird is behaving will often help in the identification process. Watch what the bird is doing and it could do you a big favour.

Birds spend a lot of time feeding and the way in which they do so can be really useful for ID purposes. Flycatchers, for example, feed in an eye-catching manner by darting out from a perch and snapping up flying insects in their beaks. Other small birds will occasionally feed in this way but are rarely as agile or persistent as the flycatchers. Similarly, there are few species that 'hawk' for flying insects as expertly or for such long periods as Swifts, Swallows and martins.

Skuas chase and harry other seabirds in an attempt to make them drop their food and obtain an easy meal. Immature gulls (a potential ID pitfall) occasionally behave in this way, but they are never as skilful as skuas in their pursuit.

Waders exhibit a variety of feeding techniques. Plovers 'run and stop', Snipe and godwits repeatedly probe their bills into the ground like sewing machines, and Turnstones live up to their name as they scuttle along the shore. Other waders have unique feeding methods. The Jack Snipe has a peculiar bobbing motion as it feeds that makes it look as if it is mounted on a set of springs, while phalaropes spin round in a circle.

Even birds that look quite similar may have different feeding methods. Unlike Redshanks, Spotted Redshanks regularly adopt a side-sweeping technique for sifting food from the water with their bills while they move along. Little Stints can be picked out from flocks of Dunlin by their much faster feeding action.

When

Picture the scene. It is January and you are visiting your local sewage works. A small bird flits into view and its small size, brownish plumage, spindly legs and thin bill tell you that it is a warbler. It looks like a Willow Warbler and behaves like a Willow Warbler, so it must be one, right? Well, it almost certainly isn't. Before you jump to conclusions based on what you have seen, it is always a good idea to think about the bigger picture and consider the time of year.

Many birds are highly seasonal in their appearances. The Willow Warbler is extremely rare in Europe in winter, but its similar relative, the Chiffchaff, is not. A closer and longer look at the bird in question reveals

ABOVE: *The Spotted Flycatcher won't win any prizes for colour, but once it darts out and snaps up an insect in its beak, its identity should become clear.*

LEFT: *It's early April and a small bird jumps off a rock and dashes across short grass, flashing a prominent white rump: a classic Wheatear encounter.*

ABOVE: A 'yellow' wagtail in
winter will be a Grey Wagtail.
Yellow Wagtails are in Africa
at this time.

few yellow tones in its plumage, dark not pale legs and, to be extra helpful, it then gives a nice, cheerful 'hweet' call, which is diagnostic of Chiffchaff.

There will always be exceptions to the norm, but most birds are where they should be at the right times of year, so don't forget to check when the peak periods are for the bird you think you have seen.

Where

Where you are is also important. A good example to illustrate this fact is the birdwatcher who sees a falcon hovering at the side of the motorway as he drives past and tells his friends he has seen a Merlin. In fact, he almost certainly saw a Kestrel. The favoured hunting habitats of the much commoner and frequently hovering Kestrel include roadside verges, where there is an abundance of small mammals for it to eat.

Some birds that look similar are found in quite different habitats. The Cormorant and Shag are a classic 'confusion pair' of species, but one where location is often the key. They are both common around much of the coast and the Cormorant is equally at home on inland waters. However, the Shag ventures inland only rarely. If you see a 'Shag' at your local reservoir, the chances are it is actually a Cormorant.

BELOW: In Britain, the Crested Tit is restricted to Scottish pine forests, but is less fussy in its choice of habitat in Continental Europe.

Some birds have restricted ranges or are fussy about their choice of habitat, rarely straying far, so the 'where' approach to bird identification can be really useful. Keep in mind the sort of birds you might expect to be at a certain place, and you will be much better prepared. It is also a good idea to ensure you have brushed up on the main identification points of these species, so you know what features you need to be looking out for before you even set out on a birdwatching trip. This is an excellent habit to get into. It never hurts to refresh your memory, especially as even the most active birders can go several years without seeing a certain species of bird.

Be aware, however, that not every bird will always be where the books say it should. For example, you might see Long- and Short-eared Owls flying over the sea as they arrive in the UK from the continent in the autumn, or a migrant Pied Flycatcher resting on a beach. I once saw a Fulmar sitting in the middle of a field 96 kilometres (60 miles) from the coast one May, when it should have been on a cliff-top nest!

FIELD GUIDES AND MAKING NOTES

What do you do when faced with a bird that you just can't name or identify with certainty? My short (and rather simple) answer to this question is to go back and look at the bird again, even more closely and for as long as you can. A common mistake made by many birdwatchers is to attempt a 'snapshot' identification, based on a brief or poor view or having noted just a couple of features that they feel should be enough to identify the bird. This frequently causes them to jump to the wrong conclusion.

Don't panic because you do not know what the bird is immediately. The longer and more carefully you watch the bird, the more chance there is of you noting important features, or of

LEFT: *The delightful Dipper (juvenile top, adult bottom) rarely strays from fast flowing streams and rivers.*

ABOVE: *Always carry a notebook in which to record your sightings and make sketches or notes of interesting or unidentifiable birds.*

it doing something or revealing a feature that makes the penny drop. Gradually piece together the information at your disposal and in this way narrow down the possibilities.

Don't make a grab for your field guide too quickly, either. It is tempting to do this, but try to resist, at least for a while. Make sure you have watched the bird for a few minutes first. In the time you spend thumbing through the pages of the book, the bird may move off and you will have wasted valuable viewing time. When you feel you've seen enough, then reach for the guide.

As you watch the bird, you may find it useful to make a few notes or produce a sketch, especially if you still can't identify it after consulting your guide. Many books tell you that you should always sketch birds you can't identify. My personal view is that this is certainly not essential, but it can help.

Don't worry about being too artistic in your efforts. This is not the time to produce a masterpiece – you may discover that you have managed to produce a perfect illustration of the bird's head and nothing else before it flies off into the distance! You can always do a neater sketch at a later stage. It is most important to fill in the main features. If you really can't draw – or simply don't want to – you can always write down what you see instead.

There are many merits to making notes in the field. You can then try to identify the bird when you get home where you have more books and time at your disposal, or you can show your efforts to someone else who may be able to offer their opinions. You have much more chance of convincing others that you have seen something unusual if you have a good field sketch made at the time of your sighting. Finally, your sketch or notes may suddenly make sense later on, after you have seen another individual of the same species or have learned something new.

Don't forget: the more experienced you become, the less often you will feel the need to make notes to identify mystery birds.

DECISION MAKING

Likely outcomes

Birds can and do turn up in strange places and behave in atypical ways, but the probability is that the bird you are watching is not rare, is in its favoured habitat and is behaving perfectly normally.

Never be too quick to leap to the conclusion that you have found something rare. If you are faced with an unfamiliar bunting that you think could be something unusual, don't just ask yourself, 'Why is this a Rustic Bunting?' Instead, ask yourself, 'Why isn't it a Reed Bunting?' Once you are sure that you have seen the bird well enough and that it is not a common species in an unfamiliar plumage, then it is time to get excited!

Trust your judgement

Every birdwatcher makes mistakes. Getting it wrong is a vital part of the learning process, so don't be disheartened when you do. Even the most experienced and well-known birders get it wrong from time to time, although they don't necessarily admit to it!

Always trust your own judgement and have faith in your observation skills. Although you can learn a lot from other birdwatchers and asking for help with identification or entering into a discussion over a mystery bird is never a bad thing, you will learn a lot more if you examine the bird in question and come to your own conclusions.

If you are not happy with an identification made by others, or disagree with what they say, keep looking. Remember: there is no such thing as an expert who is never wrong.

BELOW: *Before you claim to have seen a rare wader, such as a Pectoral Sandpiper (below right), make sure you are not looking at a juvenile Ruff (below left) – a confusingly variable, and much commoner alternative!*

2 GOING FURTHER

Birds regularly change their appearance, which makes things even more difficult for the birdwatcher. There are breeding and non-breeding plumages and a variety of other plumages inbetween. Then there is the challenge of immature birds. In the case of birds such as eagles and large gulls, it can be several years before they reach adulthood and they adopt a number of different plumages as they mature.

Identifying birds in flight and by their songs and calls can also be a daunting prospect. But don't be put off. You should persevere because if you ignore every flying bird and bird sound with which you are confronted, you will miss out on seeing – and identifying – a lot of species. And after all, it is precisely these kinds of challenges that make birds such fascinating subjects to study.

SEASONAL APPEARANCES

Some birds are much easier to identify at certain times of year than others. The breeding plumage for many species is colourful and distinctive. Most of the birds you see in spring and summer will be adult birds in this plumage, but in autumn and winter, you will encounter them in non-breeding plumage. This may be relatively drab or nondescript, and it is often more challenging to identify. At this time, you will also be confronted with a large proportion of birds that hatched during the summer, and these will be in juvenile or first-winter plumages, which may be quite different to adult plumages (see page 35).

You can become so accustomed to birds looking a certain way that they can really puzzle you at a time of year when they are in a different plumage. Ducks are notoriously difficult to identify in late summer when the ordinarily colourful drakes are in their brown, female-like 'eclipse' plumage for camouflage while they moult and replace their flight feathers. The drakes have not all mysteriously vanished: they just look very different.

OPPOSITE: *The Osprey is one of the easiest raptors to identify in flight. The contrast between its dark brown upperparts and largely white underparts is striking as it hovers above the water in search of fish.*

BELOW: *Few birds demonstrate such a dramatic difference between breeding (above) and non-breeding plumage (below) Black Guillemot.*

Always consider the time of year and what the bird in question should actually look like at that time.

Scruffy birds

You will often come across birds that look rather scruffy and do not match any of the illustrations in your field guide. The chances are they are in transition (moult) from one plumage to another.

Spotted Redshanks do not keep their superb black breeding plumage – when they are unmistakable – for long. There is only a small window of opportunity to see adult birds at their very best in North-west Europe: from about mid-May into the first half of June as northbound migrants pass through, and again in late June and July as the first birds arrive back, still in breeding condition. At other times you will see Spotted Redshanks looking blotchy and a bit of a mess, in their rather nondescript grey non-breeding plumage, or as 'dusky' juveniles, which is why they are such a confusing species.

Feathers also become worn, lose their colour through bleaching or can be lost prior to being replaced during moult. Adult birds look rather unkempt after the breeding season.

ABOVE: *The Knot's colourful breeding plumage (above) can be a puzzle if you are only used to seeing them in their winter grey (below).*

RIGHT: *Meadow Pipits look much neater in autumn (right) than in late summer (left), when the breeding season has taken its toll on their feathers.*

The smart male Redstart you saw in your local woods in early May inevitably looks very different by early August after the rigours of raising a family.

Juveniles and immatures

Any bird that is not an adult can be classed as an immature. These younger birds can look very different to adults, and you could be easily fooled into thinking that you were looking at a completely different species, so beware! Juvenile birds – those in their first set of true feathers – are a real pitfall. Many look crisp and well marked because of their complete set of fresh feathers. Gold-spangled, pale-legged, short-billed juvenile Redshanks are wrongly identified as Wood Sandpipers so many times and yet you wouldn't mistake a red-legged, adult Redshank for a Wood Sandpiper. Just one example of the curse of the confusing juvenile!

Remember, you will only see juvenile plumage for a few weeks before birds progress to their next immature plumage: 'first winter', which lasts roughly until the following spring when 'first summer' plumage is attained. By this time, many birds (especially passerines) are virtually inseparable from adults. Others still look very different at this age and have to pass through a varying

ABOVE: *Even birds of the same species and age can look very different during times of moult. Groups of adult Curlew Sandpipers typically exhibit a range of plumages in spring and autumn.*

BELOW: *Large gatherings of birds, such as this feeding flock of Scaup, will consist of several plumages to test your ID skills: males, females and a variety of different ages.*

number of subsequent plumages (depending on the species) in the same sequence of alternating 'winters' and 'summers' before they can be classed as adults.

You should also be aware of the more general terms of 'sub-adult' for the oldest immature birds and 'first year' (incorporating juvenile, first winter and first summer), 'second year' (second winter and second summer) and so on.

Many immature birds also qualify for the category of 'scruffy' birds because they boast a mixture of immature and adult feathers as a consequence of replacing only selected tracts of feathers at a time during each moult. Immature gulls, for example, usually look messy (this is why many birdwatchers ignore them!) while they gradually replace their brown and black feathers with the adult versions over a period of what can be as much as four years in the case of large gulls.

Try to work out the age of the birds you see. You will gain a lot more satisfaction if you are able to identify the Peregrine you have just seen as a first-winter male than if you simply enter a non-descriptive 'Peregrine' in your notebook. Knowing the age of a bird can also help to put the sighting into perspective.

The timing of the appearance of juvenile birds is pretty standard as most birds breed during the same period each year. As a result, you can work out when they will appear and know when you should see them. I expect to see my first juvenile Little Stint and Curlew Sandpiper of the autumn in England in the last ten days of August, but my first juvenile Dunlin of the

RIGHT: *Juvenile Kittiwakes (below) are strikingly patterned and look very different to adults (above).*

year about a month earlier. Juveniles of many long-distance migrants appear relatively late, so if you think you have seen the juvenile of a Siberian-nesting wader in North-west Europe in June or July, think again!

One day in the middle of March, I met someone who was very excited about having seen a female Garganey with a brood of ducklings. Garganey are traditionally one of the earliest summer migrants to the UK, so the sighting of a female at this time would not have been out of the question, but there is no way one would have had time to pair up, build a nest and lay, incubate and hatch eggs. Not wishing to discourage the lady, I nodded approvingly, but it was no surprise to find a brood of Mallard ducklings with their mother in the spot to which I was directed.

ABOVE: *The brown feathers among the adult grey feathers of this Hen Harrier show it is an immature male.*

BELOW: *The plumage of juvenile Little Stints always looks particularly fresh and crisp.*

THE IMPORTANCE OF SONGS AND CALLS

BELOW: *Many elusive birds give themselves away by calling or singing. The Grasshopper Warbler's 'fishing reel' song is often the first clue to its presence.*

Birds tend to be pretty vocal creatures compared to most other animals, which is good news for birdwatchers as their songs and calls are extremely useful methods of identification.

In the case of some tricky species, hearing the call or song is essential to be certain of a correct identification. For example, Marsh and Willow Tits look incredibly similar and can be hard to tell apart on sight alone. However, the emphatic, sneezing 'pitchuu' of the former is quite different from the buzzing nasal notes of the latter. Then there are the species, such as Quail and Nightingale, that you will hear many more times than you will see them. You may not notice them at all if you don't familiarize yourself with their songs.

Many birds do sound very similar and it may take a lot of practice for you to learn their songs. It takes a trained ear to separate Blackcap

RIGHT: *Flying birds are usually helpfully vocal. The Whimbrel utters a rapid series of high-pitched 'tittering' calls, which instantly separates it from the Curlew.*

top tip

The best way to learn bird sounds is to hear them for yourself. Although recordings are a great identi- fication aid, you cannot beat hearing the real thing. Field guides try to describe bird sounds, but be warned: some sounds, especially songs, simply cannot be put into words, no matter how hard the writers try.

from Garden Warbler on song alone. It took me several springs finally to get it right. Others are not so tricky. The bizarre, pig-like squeals of Water Rail cannot be confused with anything else – apart from a squealing pig, of course! The Chiffchaff and Cuckoo even sing their names to help you.

The more time you spend in the field and the more attention you pay to the sounds you hear, the more you will pick up. As with sight identification, learning the songs and calls of the commonest birds is a great starting point. You can then filter out these sounds and concentrate on the unfamiliar ones.

Try to follow up every new song or call you hear with a sighting of the bird. Even familiar birds make unusual sounds from time to time, and males and females of the same species may sound different. The far-carrying call of the male Cuckoo is one of the most familiar bird sounds, but the female's bubbling trill is easy to overlook or pass off as something else.

Learning bird sounds is one of the most difficult aspects of birdwatching, but the effort you spend doing so will be repaid a million times over as it will seriously enhance your birding experiences.

Mimics, subsongs and squeaks

Mimics are potentially an identification pitfall whenever you only hear birds without actually seeing them. A surprising number of species can mimic others or

BELOW: The short, sharp 'tek' calls of the Tree Sparrow (below) are subtly different from the familiar chirping of the House Sparrow (bottom).

ABOVE: *The Marsh Warbler is a master mimic. Its song contains phrases from the songs of many European and also many African birds to really confuse birdwatchers!*

at least steal part of their song in an attempt to make their own sound more impressive.

Starlings are probably the best-known European mimics. As well as being able to imitate sounds such as mobile phones and car alarms, they can do passable imitations of many other birds. I have heard them imitating more than 50 different species.

More than once, I have pricked up my ears thinking I have heard something good, only to find a Starling perched on a chimney pot, singing its head off. Other common European mimics include Song Thrush, Skylark, Great Tit and Reed Warbler. It is quite normal for them to adopt snatches of other bird's songs.

Another pitfall is subsong – basically a half-hearted attempt at real song that can be heard outside the breeding season or as a warm-up for the main performance in spring. Be aware, too, of the various squeaks and hisses produced by young birds in summer while they remain out of sight in dense cover.

Sometimes birds make sounds that they simply aren't meant to, so be warned and always try to get a sighting to back up your suspicion if you can, just to make sure.

FLIGHT ID

Many birds are, admittedly, extremely difficult or even impossible to identify in flight. It would take a brave birder to identify the silhouettes of high-flying finches, buntings and pipits, unless they call. Some birds, such as Waxwing and Starling, have a virtually identical flight silhouette and style despite looking completely different at rest.

On the other hand, many sightings consist of flight-only views. Then there are birds, such as seabirds and raptors, which are seen far more frequently in flight than at rest. This means that a knowledge of flight ID is essential.

Key features revealed

Here is the good news. Some birds are actually easier to identify in flight than they are on the ground. This is because

they reveal key features – especially on the wings, rump and tail – that are not usually visible when they are at rest. Ringed and Little Ringed Plovers can be difficult to separate, but they can be instantly identified in flight by the former's white wing-bars and the plain wings of the latter.

Consider another example. Picking out Velvet Scoters among a group of 5,000 Common Scoters on a choppy sea at a kilometre's range is not easy, but if the flock takes flight and the Velvets flash their gleaming white secondary feathers, they are easy to find among the mass of plain-winged Commons.

LEFT: *This female Garganey is obligingly having a stretch to reveal the pattern and colours in its wing – invaluable aids for identifying female ducks.*

OPPOSITE (CLOCKWISE FROM TOP LEFT): *The white wingbars of the Black-tailed Godwit, the black-and-white tail of the Red-breasted Flycatcher, the black axillaries of the Grey Plover and the plain wings of the Bar-tailed Godwit are key 'in flight' features to look for.*

RIGHT: *Little Terns have a seemingly endless supply of energy. They dash around at high speed, hover over water with their wings a blur and plunge in at such speed, it is a wonder they don't do themselves permanent damage!*

top tip

Flying finches are not easy to identify, but a good tip is to look closely at their rumps. These come in a variety of colours, ranging from green (Chaffinch and Greenfinch) to white (Bullfinch, Brambling and Goldfinch), yellow (Siskin and Serin), orange (Hawfinch) and red (male Crossbill and Common Rosefinch).

top tip

Watch flying birds for as long as you can. Snapshot views may give a false impression of their real flight action. Crows can soar in convincing raptor fashion for long periods before entering into their usual 'flappy' flight, while Feral Pigeons seem to have the ability to imitate momentarily virtually any bird they wish.

Underwing pattern and colour can also be important, especially if you are viewing the bird from below. Adult Little Gulls have a dark underwing and white upperwing, which gives them a contrasting 'black-and-white' appearance in flight. One of the best and most reliable ways to separate Arctic Tern from Common Tern is the 'see-through' flight feathers of the former.

Flight mode

Birds fly in an amazing number of different ways, which is helpful for ID purposes. Woodpeckers can be identified from afar by their deeply undulating flight, while the familiar 'flap, flap, glide' of the Sparrowhawk and the peculiar flickering wing beats of the Common Sandpiper are an instant give-away. Terns have a light, buoyant flight that makes them rise and fall as if they were attached to a piece of string, and shearwaters' name says it all!

Raptors have a wide variety of flight styles, ranging from the rapid, flickering wing beats of Merlin and the 'beatless' soaring of eagles to the ground-hugging hunting flight of harriers.

Shapes and silhouettes

When you are confronted with distant birds, shapes and silhouettes may be all you have to go on. However, this can often be enough for identification purposes. Most people can identify a Swift with a cursory glance, but this is not because of its plumage. Rather, it is the scythe-winged, boomerang-shaped profile that makes for instant recognition, even when the bird is circling high in the sky.

Raptors look confusingly similar when perched, but it is a different story when they take to the

ABOVE: *Little Gulls (seen here with a single Black-headed Gull) swoop down to pick insects from the surface of the water in a graceful 'dip-feeding' style – a flight mode more reminiscent of terns than gulls.*

BELOW: *The Lapwing gets its name from its 'floppy' flight and paddle-shaped wings, which produce a flash of black one moment and white the next.*

air. Once airborne their different shapes and proportions can be fully appreciated. These are features you will have to use in many raptor-viewing situations when no plumage details are visible. Likewise, experienced seawatchers can identify specks on the horizon because they are so familiar with birds' shapes and silhouettes and with the way they fly – not because they have superb eyes or optics.

The shape of birds' outstretched wings can help, too. Look to see whether they are pointed or round-tipped, long and thin, or short and broad. The relative proportions of the 'arm' (inner wing) and 'hand' (outer wing) are also worth noting. In addition, look at the way the bird holds its wings because many species have distinctive flight profiles. Harriers glide with their wings held in a shallow 'V' shape; the Osprey's kinked wings form an 'M' shape; and eagles hold their wings flat.

Back to front

Birds' tails come in a variety of shapes and sizes, so don't forget to look at the rear end of flying birds. As well as looking at the length of the tail, try to ascertain if the tip is rounded, square, forked or notched. Some birds, such as swallows, terns and skuas, have extensions to their tail in the form of tail streamers. Other birds are characterized by their apparent lack of a tail. The Woodlark has a very short tail that gives the impression someone has been at it with a pair of scissors!

ABOVE: *The distinctive 'flying cross' shape of the Gannet enables you to identify even the most distant of individuals passing by at sea.*

RIGHT: *Common Buzzards (above) and Honey Buzzards (below) are a tricky pair to separate. Remember that the latter holds its wings flat or slightly drooped in flight, while the former raises its wings in a shallow 'v'.*

top tip

A word of warning: not every flock of birds you see flying in 'V' formation will be geese. Swans, ducks, waders and gulls all fly in this way, as do many other birds from time to time.

LEFT: *You will need to pay attention to structure and flight mode with skuas, as their plumage is very similar. Shown clockwise are adult dark-phase Arctic Skua, juvenile Long-tailed Skua, juvenile Pomarine Skua and juvenile Arctic Skua.*

BELOW: *The Red Kite's deeply forked tail gives it an unmistakable flight silhouette.*

Don't ignore the front end of birds, either. Some birds show a protruding head in flight, while others can appear almost headless. Little Auks have virtually no projection at the front due to their tiny beaks and 'flat' faces, but the hawk-like head of the Cuckoo is very prominent. You may also be able to make out the size and shape of the beak. The monster, down-curved bill of a Curlew is a striking sight even when the bird is in flight.

The way in which the neck and head is carried is useful, too, as this can be diagnostic of certain species. Spoonbills, cranes and storks fly with their head and neck extended, while herons and egrets tuck their head and neck in. Corn Buntings are rather nondescript plumage-wise, but have a quirky habit of dangling their legs and feet as they fly.

SUBSPECIES

BELOW: *Until recently, the Hooded Crow was considered to be just a subspecies of the Carrion Crow even though it looks quite different!*

Many birds occur in a variety of subspecies, or races, across their range. These are different populations of the same species that may look slightly different. Sometimes only size and the brightness of the plumage separates two subspecies, and in the majority of cases, identifying these subtle variations in the field is quite difficult.

The millions of Russian Starlings that spend the winter in Western Europe are indistinguishable from 'our' own birds. However, other subspecies, such as Pied and White Wagtails, or Blue-headed and Yellow Wagtails, are readily separable.

Some field guides provide only a passing mention or a thumbnail sketch of subspecies. It is true that most will tell you that the Greenland White-fronted Goose differs from the European White-fronted Goose by its orange – not pink – bill. But there is much more to the Greenland race than that, including its darker plumage, more extensive barring below, larger bill and the fact that virtually its entire world population winters solely in Scotland and Ireland.

So if a bird looks a little different from what you expect, consider the possibility that it could be from a different population. It might just be a different subspecies from the one you are used to seeing.

BELOW: *The Brent Goose occurs in three subspecies in North-west Europe: the Black Brant (left), the dark-bellied Brent (centre) and the pale-bellied Brent (right). They are easily identifiable in the field and are considered to be separate species by some authorities.*

REAL-LIFE VIEWS

The importance of certain features can be exaggerated in field guides and in field conditions may not really be that useful. For example, the yellow rump and central crown stripe of Pallas's Warbler are often cited as key features to look for, but spotting these features on a tiny bird flitting among the leaves high in the canopy on a windy autumn day is not easy. Just because you cannot see them, it does not always mean you are not looking at a Pallas's Warbler.

BELOW: *Views of Common Scoters are often quite distant. They frequently appear as long, black straggly lines of 'dots' flying low over the sea.*

ABOVE: *Close views of Sooty Shearwaters are a real treat, but more often than not, they don't come much better than the specks on the horizon.*

BELOW: *Adult Yellow-legged Gull. Dull, flat light is best for gull watching as it enables you to accurately judge and compare the various shades of black and grey on the birds' upperparts.*

Let's take another example. The 'rings' on the tail of a female or immature male Hen or Montagu's Harrier (collectively referred to as 'ringtails') will be hard to see on many occasions. It is the white rump set against the dark brown upperparts that will catch your eye first.

Remember that the illustrations and descriptions in field guides represent perfect views of the birds in question. The views that you get in real life will often be far from ideal – don't be put off a school of thought just because you can't see everything the books say you should.

Light and shade

Natural lighting effects have the ability to transform completely the appearance of a bird. Bright sunlight, for example, has a 'bleaching' effect on plumage and can make ascertaining colours and tones very tricky. Trying to judge the colour of bare parts is particularly difficult in such conditions.

The leaves of the woodland canopy can have a neutralizing effect on greens and yellows. On one occasion, I met some birders claiming to have seen three Yellow-browed Warblers in a strip of coastal woodland on a day when only one was present. They said that one was 'dull', one looked 'normal' and one was 'very bright'. In fact, they simply saw the same bird against different backgrounds and in different light intensities throughout the course of the day.

Summing up

Don't expect to be able to identify every bird you see. If you really cannot identify a bird and be 100 percent sure of its identity, be prepared to forget about it. It is better to 'let it go' than earn yourself the dreaded reputation of being a 'stringer' – a birder who fabricates bird sightings.

You will become a much better birdwatcher if you are happy to admit defeat instead of making a rash identification. Many birders simply do not look closely enough at birds or pretend to see features that are not there, and in consequence they never learn very much about bird identification.

The more you watch birds and the more experienced you become, the more birds you will be able to identify successfully. Eventually, you will reach a point where the number of birds you can identify outnumbers those you can't, and the birds you can't identify are likely to be something rare or unusual.

LEFT: *Singing Wood Warbler. 'Dappled lighting' effects can alter the appearance of woodland birds in bright sunshine, so beware.*

FIELDCRAFT

By their very nature of being wild creatures –
especially ones that can fly – birds can be difficult to
observe. They present you with the task of finding
them in the first place and then the challenge of
obtaining good views, but birding wouldn't be the
exciting hobby it is if the birds made it too easy!
A crucial element of fieldcraft is to blend in with your
surroundings so that you become almost invisible to
birds. However, there is much more to it than that.
The way you think and the decisions you make are
integral parts of effective fieldcraft and being a good
birdwatcher. As this section of the book shows, they
will play a major role in the birds you see.

*Becoming proficient in fieldcraft will give you a much greater chance of witnessing
memorable sights, such as this juvenile Peregrine with its freshly caught prey.*

3 ESSENTIAL SKILLS

How you act while out in the field determines how successful you are as a birdwatcher. Effective use of fieldcraft will not only increase the number of birds you see, it could also mean the difference between getting prolonged, 'scope-filling views and being disappointed with a fleeting rear-view glimpse as your quarry flies off into the distance, never to be seen again.

The more you go birding and practise the skills that are part and parcel of being a good birder, the more natural watching birds will be. You will become more aware of what is happening around you, be in a good position to react in the best way to certain situations, and be able to anticipate what might happen next. As your fieldcraft improves, you should find the whole experience of birding so much more rewarding.

WHAT IS FIELDCRAFT?

A popular misconception is that birdwatchers creep around commando-style, decked out in camouflage gear and hiding in the middle of bushes for hours at a time. There is no need to take fieldcraft to such extremes to get close to birds. On the other hand, shouting to your companions while dressed in your loudest Hawaiian shirt and making yourself visible for miles around will seriously hinder your chances of being a successful birder!

Basic fieldcraft consists of simple techniques that aim to make you as unobtrusive as possible to blend in with the environment. These include speaking softly and only when really necessary, looking and listening intently, wearing neutral colours, using natural cover, and walking slowly and carefully, scanning ahead as you go. They are good habits to get into – and will certainly help you to see more birds.

Fieldcraft is also about developing an awareness of birds and the habitats in which they live, noticing as many of the birds around you as possible, knowing how different species behave, and finally, using all of this information to your advantage.

Fieldcraft does seem to be something of a dying art among modern birders. Powerful optics mean there is less of a need to stalk birds or get close to them. Many of us are guilty of 'nature

OPPOSITE: *Being alert and ready for chance sightings at all times will make you a much more successful birdwatcher.*

BELOW: *Blending in with your surroundings is a basic, but essential, piece of fieldcraft to learn.*

ABOVE: *You will need to use all your fieldcraft skills to get a view of a Dartford Warbler as good as this. 'Pishing' (see page 86) would certainly help.*

BELOW: *Despite being common birds, Jays are often wary of humans so approach with care to make sure you get a good view.*

reserve syndrome' because habitats, trails and hides are laid out so that visitors' disturbance to birds is minimal. At the biggest reserves, where the birds' every need is catered for and hides and screens conveniently disguise our outlines, birds literally parade before our eyes as if they have been trained to do so. At such times, it is tempting not to bother to use fieldcraft.

Sooner or later, you will find yourself birding in places where good fieldcraft is essential. These are the sites where you have to be at your sharpest and most 'aware' if you are to blend in and see the birds that are present. I soon learned the necessity to 'blend in' when I began to visit the Ouse Washes. The slightest hint of a bobble hat poking up above the flood banks at this very flat, very big stretch of flood meadows in the Cambridgeshire Fens ensured that every bird for a kilometre or more took flight.

It never hurts to be too cautious when birding. Always assume you are in a 'difficult' habitat and that the bird you are watching is wary, has seen you and could fly off at any minute, and act accordingly.

GETTING TO KNOW BIRDS

While you are out watching birds, try to guess where different species could be, what they might be doing or what they will do next. Just as actors try to get into the mind of the character they are playing, putting yourself in the position of the bird you are looking for can really help. It's not as silly as it sounds and you will be surprised how often it works.

I often find myself wandering around thinking: 'That bush looks good for a such and such' or 'If I was a so and so, I'd be there'. It has worked for me many times and it is a great feeling when the bird you have been thinking of suddenly appears. Go with your instincts. If a grassy paddock looks like a good spot for a migrant Ring Ouzel, then a passing migrant may well have thought the same.

Birds are creatures of habit and many will behave in exactly the same way each time you see them. Waders spend long periods feeding, warblers generally make themselves hard to see, shearwaters fly quickly past at sea, and shrikes perch in exposed places. Of course, some birds have exasperating habits. Spoonbills are well known for spending long periods asleep.

Getting to know a species' habits will greatly increase your chances of finding it. It took me a few years to see my first Lesser Spotted Woodpecker, but once I had seen a few, I realized that

ABOVE: *Chats, including the Stonechat, perch in prominent places, so don't forget to scan the tops of bushes, tall vegetation and fence posts.*

BELOW: *Lapland Buntings are often to be found in coastal stubble fields during autumn and winter where they creep around like mice and generally make themselves hard to see.*

top tip

Birds spend a lot of time feeding, so if you know what your target species likes to eat, you have a useful lead. Even species that live in the same habitat can have different diets or may frequent microhabitats such as particular trees, areas of the beach or depths of water where their favoured food is found.

RIGHT: *Black Redstarts have a liking for waste ground and built-up areas and often nest on buildings and power stations.*

they usually frequent the upper branches of trees as opposed to the main trunks. By focusing my attention in the right area, I now see this elusive species on a more regular basis.

It can really help to think back to the last time you saw a bird, and where it was and what it was doing. Over time, this will stick in your mind and you will instinctively look in a certain place and in a certain way for a particular species – and see it more often as a result.

GETTING CLOSER

It is not always easy to decide how close you can, and indeed should, get to birds. You will understandably want to get the best views possible, but approaching too closely and flushing the bird could be a disaster, as you may never see it again.

Always approach birds slowly and quietly, stop regularly to see what they are doing, and use whatever natural cover you can find to break up your outline. If the birds remain in the same place or carry on feeding or sleeping, the chances are they either haven't seen you or are not concerned with your presence.

Look for signs of alarm as you approach. Stretched necks and heads, an increase in the amount and volume of calls, birds swimming or walking away or stopping what they are doing are all signs that you are either too close or not hidden well enough! Sudden movements are the worst for spooking birds, so avoid them at all costs and always try to move smoothly.

ABOVE: *Many sightings of Merlins are brief and consist only of flight views of birds dashing past on a hunting foray.*

Disturbances spread rapidly through flocks, so be extra-careful when watching these. They usually have a 'scout' looking out for danger and ready to warn the others: don't expect to take them by surprise. Avoid flushing flocks if possible as they can be visible from afar and set off a 'domino rally' flushing effect on other birds in the vicinity.

How close you get to birds often depends on the situation in which you find them. Newly arrived migrants can be very tired and hungry. Their main concern is to rest and replenish their fat supplies by feeding vigorously. As a result, they are often very approachable and can give excellent views. Birds generally feel safer in areas they know well, but if they are forced into unfamiliar territory, they may become much warier.

Then there are the birds that you should avoid flushing at all costs. Woodpigeons and Pheasants make an almighty clatter as they fly through the trees; Grey Herons in flight can have a devastating effect on the marsh full of settled birds that you can't wait to get scanning through; and even the humble Blackbird can become your enemy with its far-carrying alarm call. If in doubt, err on the side of caution and keep your distance, at least until you have had a good view.

ABOVE: *An old name for the Redshank is 'siren of the marsh' and with good reason. This skittish wader's far carrying 'teu-du-du' and harsh alarm calls warn every bird in the vicinity of your presence if you disturb one!*

LEFT: *Feeding birds may allow close approach. Crossbills are generally unconcerned with the presence of humans as they split open larch cones in the treetops.*

top tip

The 'sit and wait' approach – letting birds come to you – has many advantages. When you are standing or sitting still, you are not making much noise and will not scare birds off with your movements. You may encounter long periods when nothing is happening, but this approach frequently pays off.

Confiding birds

BELOW: *The Dotterel's old name of 'dotty little fool' is a reflection on its remarkably confiding behaviour.*

While some birds are notoriously wary, others can be almost tame. In winter, Waxwings are usually so engrossed in gorging themselves on berries that they rarely concern themselves with human attention, even allowing approach to within a few metres. Many Arctic birds that have little contact with humans on their breeding grounds can also be very confiding. Snow Bunting, Shorelark and phalaropes fall into this category. In the majority of situations, you can approach these species closely without much fear of disturbing them or flushing them far.

Juvenile birds tend to be tamer than adults. They have had less experience of humans and are less suspicious, so they are often very approachable. A juvenile Upland Sandpiper that arrived on the Isles of Scilly one October after crossing the Atlantic actually took mealworms from the hands of delighted birders.

Hides

BELOW: *The observatory at Welney Wildfowl & Wetlands Trust Refuge in Norfolk will provide you with unforgettable close encounters with winter wildfowl.*

I have mixed views on hides. They are certainly great for letting you get close to birds as your outline is completely disguised. In many nature reserves, you have to enter hides to get to the best 'birdy' bits. But it is a myth that you need to sit in hides to see birds well. You can actually miss a lot of birds while sitting in

them because your view is so restricted. I can recall numerous incidents where birdwatchers in a hide (including myself) have missed a good bird flying right over their heads.

If I can view an area without having to go in a hide, then usually I will. Some hides are really not necessary at all and you could sit in them all day and hardly see a bird. Others open up a view that rivals anything the best nature programmes on television could produce. It is up to you to decide which ones are worth spending time in.

EFFECTIVE SITE COVERAGE

Take in the bigger picture by trying to see and hear what is happening all around you, instead of concentrating too much on one spot or group of birds. 'Being aware' in this sense is a vital piece of fieldcraft.

As you walk around a site, ask yourself which areas have the most birds, which bits look attractive to birds, where are the good areas to stop and scan, and what you can hope to see in particular spots. It is well worth stopping regularly to ask yourself these questions.

You will probably already know the answers to these questions at the places you watch regularly. If I am visiting my favourite coastal marsh on a winter's afternoon, I usually stop at the reedbed to look for Bearded Tit, scan over the marshes for a good

top tip

Cars make excellent mobile hides. If I am watching birds at the roadside, I always try to view from my car to avoid scaring off wary birds by getting out and banging the doors. In winter, it is also a lot warmer!

BELOW: *Being able to 'work' sites and different habitats is a useful piece of fieldcraft. The 'scrape' in the foreground should be scanned for wildfowl and waders, while the reedbed may produce a Bittern or Marsh Harrier in flight. The woodland behind is best tackled early in the day when the birds are most active.*

RIGHT: *The Chough is a real 'specialist' with a restricted range. It nests on steep cliffs and probes for insects in short-turf, so you will need to make sure you are looking in the right habitat when searching for this charismatic crow.*

BELOW: *Seeing elusive species such as the Golden Oriole (male and female above) and the Corncrake (bottom) requires great patience. Even then, you may have to be content with the briefest of glimpses or perhaps just flight views.*

half an hour from my favourite bench, walk down to the beach if the tide is in to look for seabirds, and then return for a second scan over the marshes, before finally watching Little Egrets, raptors and gulls coming in to roost. Then I'll wander back to the car park area and look for Woodcocks flying out at dusk. I can be pretty confident I have 'worked' the site properly by the time I leave.

Visiting sites for the first time can be very exciting, but without the sort of intimate knowledge I have just described, you may find that finding and seeing birds can be quite tough. Your challenge is to make sure that you ask yourself the right questions so that you end up finding the birds.

How long should you spend?

It is really up to you how long you spend in a particular location, but as a general rule, it is best to take your time and make sure you have looked thoroughly to allow enough time for any hidden birds to appear. In most cases, you will find there are more birds present than you at first thought. If there are plenty of birds to look through, then you obviously need to take your time until you are happy you have seen and identified everything.

I can still recall the disappointment I felt as a young birdwatcher on a particular occasion when I left a hide too early. A bit later, I bumped into the people I had left in the hide and was entertained with the tale of the Kingfisher that had flown in and proceeded to fish in front of the hide for half an hour. At the time, I had never seen a Kingfisher and it was my most-wanted bird. It still smarts, even today, hundreds of Kingfishers later.

On another occasion, I had been sitting in the famous Daukes Hide at Cley in North Norfolk for over an hour, patiently scanning through the birds on the scrapes, before eventually leaving in search of a Pectoral Sandpiper that had been seen elsewhere on the reserve. On arrival home, I learned that a Black-winged Pratincole had flown in seconds after I left. Sometimes you just can't win, no matter how hard you try!

There are certain birds for which you will have to put in more time. Searching for raptors generally requires a lengthy wait, and naturally elusive birds such as crakes, rails and game birds will more often than not need a bit of extra effort. If, on the other hand, you keep seeing the same Robin and Dunnock over and over again, it is generally time to move on.

Circuit training

Flocks of birds moving through cover usually have fixed feeding 'circuits', so if you wait in one spot, the flock is likely to pass through at some point. Individual birds can act in this way, too, and instead of trying to keep up with a mobile bird, it often pays to take this easy approach. Birds consistently follow feeding patterns and you can really use this to your advantage.

You can also perform your own 'circuits' to make sure you give yourself the maximum chance of seeing birds. Plan your route to

LEFT: *Flocks of tits are very vocal and invariably have other species tagging along in the search for food.*

ensure you cover as much of a site as possible, but try to avoid retracing your steps. If you return to an area that you have already walked through, you may find there is a lot less bird activity the second time around because the birds have been disturbed.

LOCATING BIRDS

Never underestimate the power of the naked eye. You will be surprised how many birds you notice without having to use binoculars because your eyes have a naturally wide field of view and excellent light-gathering ability. You may not be able to identify the birds this way, but you can then reach for your optics.

In the majority of birding situations, it is your binoculars that you will use for scanning over an area, initially identifying birds and making sure you get a good sighting before they disappear. You can then reach for your telescope for better, close-up views or if the bird is so far away that you can't identify it with binoculars alone. Do make sure you get a good binocular view before

BELOW: Bare trees are full of distinctive features. Forks, knots, and obvious individual branches can be invaluable when it comes to getting onto the birds that are sitting in them.

reaching for your telescope. It is highly frustrating to try to locate a bird in your 'scope first – and fail to get on it at all!

This is an easy mistake to make with birds in flight. Flying birds are much easier to locate in binoculars than in a telescope because of binoculars' wider field of view. With practice, you will find getting birds in your 'scope much easier. It is worth practising on common birds and honing your 'locating' skills, so you are ready for that once-in-a-lifetime moment when a Black-browed Albatross flies past during a seawatch!

Spotting a bird with the naked eye and then homing in on it with optics can be tricky, though. The view changes dramatically once everything is magnified and the field of view narrows. A good tactic to adopt is to use obvious objects around you to help locate birds. There will always be some kind of natural or artificial feature to help you out. A buoy on the sea, that dead tree on the horizon, or even other birds. The islands on the famous 'scrape' at Minsmere, Suffolk, are actually numbered to make it really easy for you!

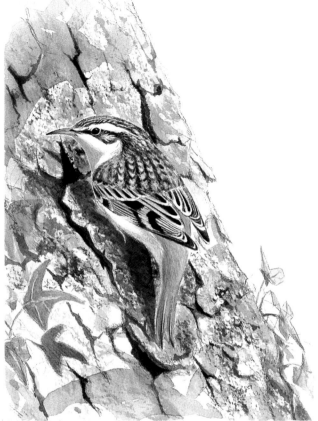

ABOVE: *The 'jerky' movement produced by Treecreepers as they shin up the sides of tree trunks will often catch your eye in woodland.*

Birds in and among trees and bushes can be very difficult to locate with binoculars. Try starting in the middle by locating the main trunk and then work your way up or down and outwards, counting the branches as you go to lead you to the bird.

Birds flying high in the sky are among the most difficult of all to locate, especially in a telescope. Watch for when they appear over obvious landmarks on the horizon or near to clouds. You can then scan straight up from the landmark or follow the shape of the clouds in your telescope to lead you to them.

Telescopes are necessary for locating birds over long distances. If you have a zoom eyepiece, make sure you set it to a low magnification to increase light gathering ability and to give you a wider field of view for initially picking birds up. You can always zoom up if you do spot something interesting and want to check out the finer details.

ABOVE: *A perfect open land-scape for a raptor watch with ample scanning opportunities over scattered woodland, open ground and a distant ridge. The weather looks ideal too!*

Scan, scan and scan again

Always scan over an area several times as you will almost certainly not see all of the birds present with just one sweep of your bins or telescope. Birds may be hidden behind all kinds of things – even other birds. It is easy to scan across a rough sea and see nothing, only to repeat the process a second time and find a

RIGHT: *You will need to search the water's edge carefully to make sure you don't overlook unobtru-sive birds like the Water Pipit.*

top tip

Take regular breaks during long spells of scanning to avoid eyestrain. What could be more frustrating than scanning intensively for Honey Buzzard over a distant wood for two hours and then suffering from 'cross-eyes' when one does appear in view so that you can't focus on it properly?

hatful of birds. Waves and troughs conceal birds on the sea remarkably well, and seaducks, grebes, divers and auks all dive regularly so they can be out of view more often than they are on the surface. The same applies to diving birds on fresh water.

Instead of scanning constantly, leave an interval between each 'sweep' to allow birds to reposition themselves or to appear on the edge of vegetation or the water's surface. New birds will probably fly in or past you while you are scanning, so the more 'sweeps' you perform, the more chance you have of seeing birds.

Looking for raptors requires a lot of scanning. They take flight only when it suits them and you will often be in for a long wait before your quarry appears. Systematic scanning of the sky and a lot of patience are the recipe for success.

Are you listening?

Hearing birds and being able to recognize and interpret the sounds they make is vital. As a rule birds are very vocal, and even when they are not singing, they call regularly for a variety of reasons, such as when alarmed or to keep in contact with others. Think how many more birds you hear than you actually see during spring and summer.

ABOVE: *Long-tailed Ducks dive for long periods and are often found on rough seas, so scan with care.*

BELOW: *A telescope will open up so many birding opportunities for you, so practise with it until using it becomes second nature.*

As an experiment, try wandering around a wood, ignoring everything you hear, and see how many silent birds you actually come across by chance. Then repeat the walk and follow up the sounds you hear to lead you to the birds making the noise. I can guarantee you will see so much more the second time around.

Spending as much time listening for birds as you do looking will pay dividends. Stop regularly to listen so you know what birds are in the area. Hearing calls can also reveal the presence of a bird long before you see it, enabling you to have your binoculars poised ready for a sighting. This is especially relevant for birds flying over – their calls act as early warning systems to tell you a bird is on its way.

Try to learn as many calls as you can. You will see so many more birds if you do. Several times I have been out at the coast and a Lapland Bunting has flown over, calling emphatically, and I've turned to the birders nearby to share my excitement only to find them looking in totally the opposite direction, having not even registered the call.

ABOVE: *The Kingfisher's high-pitched, piping calls can reveal its presence long before you see it, so listen carefully and have your bins at the ready.*

RIGHT: *Use your ears just as much as your eyes when bird-watching. Cupping your hands behind your ears is a useful – and very effective – technique for amplifying bird sounds.*

A HELPING HAND

It is always worth watching the behaviour of birds closely – even if they are not a particularly interesting species – as they will occasionally lead you to something special.

Roosting owls are not welcomed in the territories of smaller birds and mixed 'gangs' team up to scold and attempt to scare off the intruder. This is bad news for the owl, but not for birders! Listen out for loud and persistent alarm-calling by birds such as tits, Chaffinches and Blackbirds and head in the direction of the calls. They could well lead you to a memorable, close encounter with a sleepy owl.

Raptors cause a commotion whenever they appear, so keep an eye out for disturbances among gatherings of potential prey. Birds will usually spot an approaching raptor long before you do. You won't always strike gold – large gulls, herons and even aeroplanes and microlights can have a similar effect – but you just might, so it is always worth looking hard when a commotion breaks out.

I have a flock of Brent Geese to thank for helping myself and a group of friends find a newly arrived White-tailed Eagle in

ABOVE: *Always be listening for calls that can reveal the presence of birds flying over. You wouldn't want to miss this flock of Snow Buntings.*

top tip

Keep an eye on Crows. These cocksure birds dive-bomb perched raptors and mob them while they fly, cawing emphatically until they are satisfied that the unwanted predators are far enough away. This behaviour can draw your attention to previously unseen raptors.

RIGHT: *Blue Tits have a knack of being the first bird to spot an approaching Sparrowhawk. Listen for their trilling alarm call, wait a few seconds and then scan the sky. You will be surprised how often a Sparrowhawk sails into view.*

BELOW: *An approaching Peregrine rarely goes unnoticed by other birds.*

Norfolk one November morning. The croaking calls of the geese suddenly reached fever pitch and the flock literally exploded into the air in a blind panic. Admittedly, White-tailed Eagles are hardly the most unobtrusive of birds, but it was the Brents' reaction that enabled us to be the first to spot the approaching giant.

Swifts, Swallows and martins can help you to see Hobbies. They rapidly scatter in all directions at the approach of one of these high-speed hunters, and their frantic, intense alarm calls often precede the arrival of a Hobby in search of a quick snack. Peregrines set their sights a little higher in terms of the size of their prey and they really do cause a stir when on the hunt. If the sky suddenly becomes filled with wheeling masses of waders, or Woodpigeons or ducks take flight in

ABOVE: *The stuff of dreams for birders. A white-phase Gyr Falcon homes in on a flock of Black-tailed Godwits, Curlews and a Redshank.*

their droves, one of these exciting raptors could well be the culprit.

Try to follow the progress of the disturbance – birds for a good kilometre or more may take to the air – and try to pinpoint exactly where the raptor is and the direction in which it is travelling. Sometimes, Peregrines will strike directly from above, so don't forget to look up as well.

What to wear

Many books on birdwatching set out strict guidelines for what you should and shouldn't wear in the field. Personally, I don't think it is that important, but there a few points worth bearing in mind.

It is not always easy to decide what to wear when birdwatching in North-west Europe, but always think 'comfort first'. If you are worrying because your boots are too tight, your hands are too cold, or because your feet are wet and you have no spare socks, you will certainly not be at your sharpest or be enjoying the experience much.

ABOVE: *Dress appropriately for each season and find a comfortable method for carrying your optics so that they are ready for use at a moment's notice.*

Think ahead before you set out and dress accordingly. The sight of birdwatchers walking along a bone-dry path in the middle of summer wearing thermals and wellington boots always brings a smile to my face! Ask yourself where you will be going and what the conditions – especially underfoot – may be like. Remember that the weather can change quickly and that the temperature can fluctuate over the course of a day. I have clothing for all weathers in the boot of my car, just in case, and always wear a hat in winter as most of the heat you loose from your body escapes through the head.

Finally, treat your hands with respect and wear a suitable pair of thin but warm gloves. Frozen fingers and cumbersome gloves are the last thing you need when it comes to operating focus wheels and tripods and writing notes.

Never stop looking

Being a birdwatcher should be a full-time occupation. Never stop looking and listening for birds, no matter where you are.

LEFT: *The Firecrest is a gem of a bird that you could find in woodland and scrub almost anywhere at any time if your luck is in.*

BELOW: *Ring Ouzels are always exciting birds to see. Shown here are first winter (top left), adult male (top right) and adult female (bottom).*

You never know what may appear next. Use fieldcraft all the time and soon it will become second nature to you.

Be ready for chance sightings. I have found good birds in the most unlikely places and in some truly bizarre situations. I have seen Waxwings from a bus window while travelling to college one day, a Ring Ouzel while doing the gardening, a flock of migrating Arctic Terns while cycling through the middle of a town far from any water, and an Alpine Swift that flew in off the sea while I was seawatching.

4 SPECIALIST SKILLS

Birdwatching will provide you with a wide variety of experiences and take you to many places. You will visit a number of different habitats and each requires you to use particular skills to 'work' them effectively and find their birds. Some require very precise fieldcraft to get the most from them.

There are also more specialized forms of birding, which can provide some of the most exciting and rewarding experiences of all. Seawatching, visible migration watching and scouring large flocks for rarities can prove to be highly addictive, so be warned!

Try to visit as many habitats as you can on a regular basis and try as many types of birding as you can – I guarantee you will see more birds if you do.

MAKING THE MOST OF HABITATS

Some places always seem to be teeming with birds, which will generally present themselves easily to you. Marshes, lakes and reservoirs are excellent places to watch birds, and there will usually be plenty of 'obvious' species to see. Other habitats are a bit more difficult to work and will require extra effort for you to get the most from them.

Reedbed birding

Reedbeds are one of the most difficult of all habitats to work. There is so much cover for birds to disappear into and many reedbed residents are specially equipped to remain hidden and act as unobtrusively as possible. Reedbeds are also home to a relatively small number of rather specialist birds. One thing is for sure: you need plenty of patience.

The best way to work a reed-bed is to find a suitable place to stand or sit so that you have a good all-round view. Many reedbed specialists will only be seen in flight so you need to be able to pick them up as soon as possible before they drop back down again. Reedbeds often contain channels and pools. If possible, position yourself so that you are looking down or over one of these mini features. Birds such as Bittern, Bearded Tit and Water Rail often appear on the edges of the reeds to feed, so scan regularly along the margins.

RIGHT: *Choose a still day, be patient and listen carefully: three of the key elements of a successful reedbed watch.*

OPPOSITE: *North-west Europe is blessed with a tremendous variety of habitats. Each one will bring you into contact with a different selection of birds.*

top tip

In enclosed habitats such as woods or scrub, telescopes are often a cumbersome inconvenience, so it is always worth having a think about whether you will really need your 'scope before you set off.

A reedbed may seem lifeless at first glance, but maintain a patient vigil on its edge and keep your eyes and ears peeled and it should reveal some of its secrets.

Woodland and scrub

Good use of fieldcraft is never more important than when birding in woodland and scrub. The golden rules are to be as quiet as you can and to take your time. Rushing around and trying to cover as much ground as possible will certainly mean you miss a lot of birds, while the noise you make will scare them away.

Walk softly, with a 'heel to toe' movement if possible to avoid crunching fallen leaves and snapping twigs. Approach corners and 'blind spots' carefully to avoid disturbing birds that might be feeding on the ground. Stopping at regular intervals to look and listen will give you a good overview of what is happening around you. You will hear many woodland birds long before you see them.

Small birds can be highly concentrated outside the breeding season, and many species band together in mixed feeding flocks. It is a bit like searching for hidden treasure. Locate the flock and

ABOVE: *Bitterns can be so well camouflaged against the reeds that they may only become visible when they move.*

BELOW: *Birding in mature woodland can be a real challenge – especially when the leaves are on the trees.*

you will be rewarded. Fortunately, these flocks create a lot of noise as the birds keep in contact with each other. Listen for the collective calls of tits and try to follow the sound until you locate the flock. The tricky part is then keeping up with the fast-moving gathering. Try to get ahead of the flock when you hear it approaching and let the birds pass through in front of you so that you can check through the birds and, hopefully, find the hidden gem tagging along.

Coniferous woodland may seem devoid of birds at first. Because it is so dense and shady, and supports a smaller variety and quantity of food than deciduous woodland, there are usually fewer birds and perhaps just a handful of coniferous 'specialists' to see. Once again, this means you will have put in extra effort.

ABOVE: *You will often hear woodland birds before you see them. Listen out for the piercing 'kik' and mechanical 'drumming' of the Great Spotted Woodpecker.*

LEFT: *Good fieldcraft is essential if you are to enjoy successful woodland birding.*

top tip

Always look on the bright side. Small birds often choose to feed on sunlit edges of bushes and trees where it is warmer and there are more insects.

Getting the most from estuaries

Estuaries can provide you with some truly memorable birding, but you must plan ahead to avoid disappointment. The most important pieces of fieldcraft for estuary watching are getting the timing of the tide right and making sure you are positioned in the right place. During the highest tides, all of the waders on an estuary can be forced off their feeding grounds and may gather in remarkable concentrations while waiting for the tide to go back out. At low tide, on the other hand, you may struggle to see any birds at all. Consulting a tide table before you go is a must.

Estuary watching is the perfect example of letting the birds come to you. Anticipate where they will gather to sit out the high tide period – usually land that remains uncovered or is higher-lying than the rest – and you should have all the birds within range. However, bear in mind that the birds can be so closely packed that picking out individual birds, let alone something unusual, can be incredibly difficult at high-tide roosts. Most birds also go to sleep, thus hiding their bills and

faces. This is not helpful as the bill is one of the key features for wader ID.

Try to be present before and after high tide. As the birds are being pushed in by the tide, they are concentrated, allowing you to scrutinize them, but remember that you will have to be quick as they are soon moved on by the tide. The period just after high tide, when the first parts of the mudflats have been uncovered, is also an excellent time for watching. The birds do not have the pressure of the incoming tide to worry about and they often remain in view for a long time, feeding in the suitable wet mud before dispersing over the mudflats.

top tip

Getting the tide right is essential if you intend to visit the coast for watching seaducks, grebes and divers or if you are planning a seawatch. The birds will be much further away at low tide. In some places, the sea goes out so far, you will have trouble seeing it, let alone any birds!

TACKLING FLOCKS

As the famous saying goes, birds of a feather flock together, and this habit is good news for birdwatchers. Large gatherings of birds look impressive and are great to watch. However, despite the popular saying, flocks are often made up of different species. This provides the opportunity to pick out something unusual.

Some species of birds, such as waders, ducks and geese, which are found in flocks outside the breeding season, pick up stragglers of other species whose range they may cross at some point. The birds they pick up act in exactly the same way as their 'carriers' and may then follow their every move – including following

BELOW: *The white-phase Snow Goose in this flock of Pink-footed Geese shouldn't take much finding, but the Tundra Bean Goose (at the rear of the group in the front left-hand corner with its head up) is a much trickier option.*

them on their migration routes. Lone and lost birds also tend to seek out flocks of their nearest relatives for security. Any flock of birds has the potential to contain something special, so you should always search with care. It is not just about wetland birds. Many passerines form flocks outside the breeding season and you should always check these carefully, too.

Some flocks of birds can be pretty daunting, but don't be put off. If you are confronted with a large gathering or flock of birds, then take your time. The time spent scanning and searching could well pay off.

Pick the best position for a good clear view without scaring the birds. Scan through, starting at the extreme left or right side of the flock. Systematically working through a flock in this way is much more effective than just looking at random areas. Once you have worked through once, scan back through from the other way. Take your time as you scan. Parts of the flock and individual birds will often be hidden; perhaps by natural features such as islands, trees or mounds of earth, but also by other birds.

As you scan, look for variations in the monotone pattern of birds and let your eyes be 'stopped' by something different: the grey mantle of a drake Scaup among Tufted Ducks, the orange of a Brambling among a flock of Chaffinches, or the whiteness of a Roseate Tern among a flock of Common Terns.

BELOW: *The rich mahogany colour, white undertail and white eye of this drake Ferruginous Duck (second left) should ensure it stands out from its Pochard companions – but only if you scan carefully!*

If I am searching for Mediterranean Gulls in a big flock of Common and Black-headed Gulls in winter, I look at the birds' heads. Mediterranean Gulls of all ages at this time have a distinctive black 'pirate's patch' behind the eye and thicker bills than Black-headed Gulls. The paler upperparts of the Mediterranean Gull are a much less eye-catching feature. If I am searching for 'white-winged' gulls (Iceland and Glaucous Gulls) among a gathering of Herring Gulls and black-backed gulls, then I look at the other end of the bird: the wingtips. The pure white tips shine like a beacon among the mass of black wingtips, even over great distances and in dull late afternoon light.

If I am scanning a flock of dark-bellied Brent Geese, hoping for a stray pale-bellied Brent Goose or a Black Brant from North America, then I concentrate on the flank and belly area. The extensive creamy-white bellies of pale-bellied Brents make them stand out from the muddy brown colours of the dark-bellied Brents, and the pure white flank patch of Black Brants contrasts strongly with the rest of their black plumage.

Looking for the most obvious features in this way will speed up the process of searching through a flock and will give you a better chance of finding something unusual among the mass of bodies. You may develop your own styles and preferred key features to look for in particular flocks. Some may work better for you than others, so have a go and see.

ABOVE: *Pay close attention to the heads of Yellow Wagtails as you scan through a flock and you may be rewarded with something more unusual. The Blue-headed Wagtail (second left) is a scarce passage migrant in Britain.*

top tip

As you scan through a flock of birds, have the possibilities of what species the flock may contain in the back of your mind, so you know what features in particular to be looking out for.

SEAWATCHING

ABOVE: *Land's End, Cornwall.*
The South-west coast of England
is one of Europe's premier sea-
watching spots. Large numbers
of Cory's and Great Shearwaters
pass by in some autumns.

Seawatching traditionally has a bad reputation among birdwatchers that don't do it often or have never enjoyed great success. The very mention of the word can conjure up mental images of being huddled on a beach staring at a birdless sea with a howling wind distributing sand and sea spray in all manner of unwanted places. However, it doesn't have to be like this, and after reading this mini guide to seawatching, I hope you will become a convert or at least be inspired to give it a try. One good seawatch and you may well be hooked for life. I know I was.

Seawatching generally refers to watching migrating seabirds passing a particular fixed point on the mainland. The star prizes are skuas, shearwaters, petrels and the ocean-going Sabine's Gull, but you can see all manner of birds, from waders and wildfowl to divers, terns, auks and grebes. Late summer and autumn provide the main period of passage and the chance of seeing the largest numbers of individual birds and species (including all of the sought-after specialities mentioned above). There is also a lighter and less predictable passage of seabirds in spring.

Unsettled weather out to sea and strong onshore winds bring seabirds closer to shore, so watching during, or just after, such conditions usually produces the best results. Precise conditions for the best results vary from region to region, so you will need to work out the best weather for observing seabirds on your part of the coast. Alternatively, why not ask the seawatching stalwarts at your local headland?

On the right day, at the right time and in the right conditions, seawatching can be tremendously exciting. All manner of birds stream past, often in considerable numbers, and there is the added attraction of having no idea what may appear next. It is also a good form of easy birding as you wait for the birds to come to you and don't have to move from one spot all day.

Are you sitting comfortably?

Comfort is essential, as you will need to sit in the same position for long periods to allow time for birds to pass. The hardened seawatchers at England's premier seawatching spot – the towering cliffs of Flamborough Head on the Yorkshire coast – watch for 14

top tip

Give your eyes a break at regular intervals and stretch your legs by going for a short walk, but always remain in earshot of fellow seawatchers. You don't want to wander off and miss the 'biggie'.

OPPOSITE BELOW: *On the right day, seawatching is hard to beat for sheer excitement as a variety of seabirds stream past.*

BELOW: *A telescope is essential for seawatching, as is choosing a suitable and comfortable vantage point.*

hours a day during the autumn, but this is taking it to extremes! I often have a session from dawn to mid-morning as seabird passage often peaks at this time, and then go for a break or go somewhere else when the passage slows down. I usually return for an afternoon watch as passage can pick up again then. Try to find some natural cover to protect you and your optics from sea spray and the wind. There is no harm in taking a cushion or even a folding chair to sit on. This will seriously improve your staying power.

Some people scan with binoculars to locate passing seabirds and then switch to their telescope to identify them, but if the passage is particularly heavy, you will become a nervous wreck if you try to keep up in this way. I always use my telescope set on a low magnification (usually 30x) when I am seawatching. Birds often pass at a certain range and along the same flight path at a particular location. By staying focused on the same area, using the same magnification, you will discover that you not only get onto most of the birds relatively easily, but also become accustomed to the relative sizes of the different species that are passing.

You can just wait and let the birds pass through your telescope, but I tend to scan round in the direction the birds are coming from and then follow them as they pass by to give me more watching and identification time.

One final word on seawatching: there is no way you will identify every bird you see at first, so just concentrate on the close ones. The more distant birds can wait a while.

ABOVE: *A view of an adult Long-tailed Skua like this one makes all the waiting on a seawatch worthwhile!*

OPPOSITE BOTTOM: *Gulls can be beautiful too as demonstrated by this stunning breeding plumaged Mediterranean Gull: always a prize find.*

GULL WATCHING

The sight of a blizzard of hundreds of gulls pouring into their roost is enough to see many birders packing up their telescope and heading for home. Gulls simply aren't the most popular of birds and I believe it is because people often don't get good views of them (and because, admittedly, gulls are hard to identify).

Evening roosts provide a great chance for you to find something unusual among the masses as they settle on the water and also to familiarize yourself with the different plumages of the commoner species. It is really exciting and rewarding to pick out a rarer species such as a Yellow-legged Gull or a 'white-winged' gull. The bigger the roost, the better your chance of doing so.

The gull population of an area can change dramatically in

top tip

When tackling large gull roosts, scan with binoculars as the birds fly in, then systematically work through the settled birds on the water from time to time with a telescope.

even a short space of time and birds regularly commute between different roosts and feeding areas, so you will be confronted with a slightly different collection of gulls each time you visit a roost. Even if you don't find anything unusual, the sight of so many birds is pretty spectacular. Most large bodies of water have a roost or at least a pre-roost where gulls collect to bathe and preen before flying to a nearby main roost that they occupy through the night, so why not get down to your local one and give it a go. You might be surprised how much you enjoy it.

Rubbish tips are also among the best places to observe gulls. You do not have to go clambering around the tip to see them, and you would almost certainly be told to leave if you did! When gulls are not feeding among our weekly rubbish and dodging the waste-turning tractors, they loaf in the surrounding fields and provide excellent viewing opportunities. If this still doesn't appeal, then take a trip to the beach, especially if there is a sewage outfall or a power station's warm-water outlet nearby.

ABOVE: *Rubbish tips may not look (or smell) nice, but they are excellent places for watching gulls and finding rarer species.*

VISIBLE MIGRATION WATCHING

Looking up is just as important as searching for birds at ground level. In some Scandinavian countries where migration takes place on a large scale overhead, birders spend most of their time scanning the skies, looking and listening for 'visible' migrants. You could do a lot worse than to follow their example. On more occasions than I care to remember, I have heard people bemoaning the lack of birds when there has been a spectacular overhead passage. They were too engrossed with scanning the bushes around them to notice.

Watching visible migration is essentially seeing and recording birds passing fixed points on land. It is really the land-based equivalent of seawatching and can be just as exciting. During spring and especially late autumn, huge numbers of birds such as finches, thrushes, buntings and pipits pass overhead through North–west Europe en route to their breeding or wintering grounds.

The coast is an excellent place to witness this phenomenon as newly arrived migrants follow the line of the coastline, but river valleys and hills are used as flyways by birds moving inland to their final destinations.

ABOVE: 'White-winged' gulls, such as this first-winter Iceland Gull, are incredibly obvious in flight.

BELOW: Keep your eyes and ears peeled and have your bins at the ready. Visible migrants tend to move straight through on a set path and in a particular direction, so you will need to be quick!

top tip

Choose a spot with a clear all-round view and with as little background noise as possible that might otherwise drown out the calls of birds flying over. Get in position early: visible migration often peaks in the first couple of hours after dawn. Light winds are a vital ingredient and a head wind can cause birds to fly lower.

October is the peak month of migration in many places and it is a great time for witnessing migration in action. Arrivals on some days can be truly spectacular, with flocks of Starlings stretching as far as the eye can see, groups of Brambling 'tekking' and 'wheezing' overhead and all manner of species whizzing through. Then there are the surprises. I have enjoyed Rough-legged Buzzard and Richard's Pipit on more than one of my visible migration watches.

You will get the most pleasure out of visible migration watching if you know your bird calls, but even if you don't you can marvel at the sheer scale of the movement and observe migration actually in progress. You certainly don't need to be able to recognize all the birds you see. It is also a good opportunity to practise and learn flight calls, as overhead migrants are usually very vocal.

ABOVE: *Fieldfares arrive from Scandinavia in droves in late autumn. 16,000 once passed over my head during a two-hour visible migration watch one October morning!*

BELOW: *All manner of birds can be seen migrating overhead, including a variety of finches. Listen for the ringing 'tsoo' calls of Siskins as they whizz over.*

SNEAKY TRICKS

Birding can often be a frustrating pastime, so there is no harm in employing a few sneaky tricks from time to time to make the task of seeing birds easier. Here are a few of my favourites that really do work.

1 The benefits and effectiveness of 'pishing' should never be underestimated. If you are not familiar with this bizarre-sounding practice, pishing is producing squeaking sounds by pursing your lips together and sucking on the back of your hand to attract small birds. Another technique, which can also bring success, is to actually make a repeated 'pish-pish-pish' sound. The birds seem to respond out of curiosity because they think the sound is the alarm call of another bird that has found a predator, and they approach to see what all the fuss is about.

Pishing is a great way to tempt skulking species out of cover if you know they are there, but it can also be worthwhile to try it just on the off-chance. I once found a Barred Warbler by

BELOW: *It is possible to attract the attention of owls by imitating the 'squeaking' of small mammals with pishing.*
I have enjoyed breathtaking views of Barn and Short-eared Owls (below) in this way.

attempting a 'pish'. There is no way I would have seen the bird if I hadn't tried my luck. Some birds respond better than others, but small birds such as warblers and crests tend to be most inquisitive and regularly respond to pishing, sometimes rewarding you with close-up views.

2 Watching gulls can be hard work, but there is one really sneaky 'cheat' to attract them. If straining your eyes in the half-light at the local reservoir roost or braving the unsavoury sights and smells of the local rubbish tip are not your thing, simply arm yourself with a loaf of bread.

Gulls are bold, brash birds and are not backwards at coming forwards when a free handout is on offer. Rare and unusual gulls are no different, and they may be attracted by the gathering mass of commoner gulls. Beaches and parks are good places to try your luck as they usually have gulls loafing around, as it were. I have attracted and fed Laughing, Ring-billed, Iceland and Mediterranean Gulls in this way: a bargain for the price of a loaf of bread.

ABOVE: Goldcrests respond particularly well to pishing and can approach to within touching distance – a wonderful experience.

3 Woodpeckers are known for their habit of drumming on trees to mark the boundaries of their territory and to attract potential mates. When you are next down in the woods, especially in spring, find a solid stick, a hollow tree or branch and a prime area of woodpecker habitat – and bang away. As you do, keep an eye on the branches above as you may just attract an inquisitive woodpecker that thinks there is an intruder in its territory. I have attracted Lesser Spotted Woodpeckers on more than one occasion in this way.

4 The Jack Snipe is a 'bogey bird' for many birdwatchers. It is actually quite a widespread winter visitor to North-west Europe, but its habit of remaining hidden among waterlogged vegetation and a reluctance to take flight mean that seeing one by conventional means is not an easy task.

Make sure you have a pair of wellington boots with you in winter when birding, as a careful 'slosh' around marshy ground and the edges of your local water bodies could well startle a Jack Snipe (or several) into making a short flight from literally at your feet. They almost always drop straight back in a few metres away so the risk of excessive disturbance is minimal.

5 WHERE AND WHEN

'Being in the right place at the right time' is a phrase that could have been made for birdwatching. Getting your timing right can mean the difference between experiencing a memorable day or the heartbreak of missing the bird of your dreams. We have all heard the words: 'You should have been here five minutes ago' or 'It was crawling with migrants last week', and felt like telling the 'helpful' birder to shut up!

A large amount of good fortune is involved is seeing birds, but you can play a big part in what you see, by giving a bit of thought to where you go and when you go there. Choosing your destination carefully and ensuring you are there at the right time is an extremely useful piece of fieldcraft. Get it right and you could enjoy the day of a lifetime.

THE BIRDING CALENDAR

The birding year in North-west Europe is incredibly varied, which is one of the major reasons why it is such as exciting region in which to watch birds. Every season and even month has its own attractions and subtle variations, so making the most of them and knowing what to look out for is a key part of successful birdwatching.

It is no good setting out to enjoy the spectacle of large flocks of wild geese in the middle of summer or getting up early in the hope of experiencing the dawn chorus in winter, even if you are the best birdwatcher in the world! The guide below is by no means comprehensive, but I hope it will give you a taste of each of the seasons and what they have to offer, as well as helping you to make the most of the birdwatching opportunities at various times throughout the year.

WINTER

Winter is one of my favourite times of year. Millions of birds flock to North-west Europe at this time, providing exciting birding and spectacular sights. Huge numbers of wildfowl, waders and gulls

OPPOSITE: *Many birds are seasonal in their appearances. Summer visitors, such as the House Martin, are only present for about half of the year.*

BELOW: *The handsome Shorelark is a highly sought-after winter visitor to the coast.*

89

take up residence after escaping harsher climes further north.
Wetlands teem with birds and are ideal locations for a day's
birding in winter. Coastal waters are just
as busy, and there are large gatherings of
seaducks, divers and grebes in the
food-rich, shallow seas around the
coast. The sight of a cloud of
Knot swirling over an estuary, a
sky full of skeins of wild
geese stretching as far as the
eye can see, and the evocative
calls of Bewick's and
Whooper Swans are the
essence of winter birding.

It is not just about wetlands
and water birds, though. As
well as common winter
visitors such as Fieldfare,
Redwing and Brambling, there
are scarcer gems such as Shorelark,
Waxwing and Snow and Lapland Buntings.
Populations of hard-to-see resident birds, such as Woodcock,
Long- and Short-eared Owls and Bittern, are swollen by arrivals
from Northern Europe and these species become more
widespread and easier to find as a result. There are local
movements, too. Birds such as Twite, Stonechat and raptors
move down from the uplands to productive feeding grounds in
the milder lowlands.

ABOVE: Waxwings are commoner in some winters than others, but are rarely found far from an ample supply of red berries.

RIGHT: Winter specialities, such as the Smew, especially the 'cracked porcelain' drakes (left), are well worth braving the cold for.

LEFT: *Finches flock together during winter. Look for Lesser Redpolls in alder and birch woodland.*

The downside of winter birding is that time is precious. The rule of spending your time wisely is never more important than during short winter days.

In winter many birds are in flocks or roost communally, so they are easier to pin down. When large numbers of birds are present, the chance of finding something unusual increases, so winter is a great time to find a flock and spend some time scanning through to see what you can turn up (see pages 77–9). Flocks of geese can contain all kinds of stragglers that they have picked up. I have spotted more than a dozen species among flocks of Icelandic Pink-footed Geese. Even the feral Greylag and Canada Geese at your local reservoir may attract stray, genuinely wild geese.

Flocks of ducks may also contain oddities, from local scarcities such as Scaup and Smew, to American vagrants such as Ring-necked Duck, American Wigeon and Green-winged Teal that have joined up with their closest relatives here. Search with care!

Large gatherings of gulls are always worthy of investigation, and never more so than in winter. Small numbers of Iceland and Glaucous Gulls associate with the large numbers of commoner species.

In winter there are few leaves on the trees and hedgerows, so seeing birds in woodland becomes easier. The birds that are present will generally show well and give themselves up relatively

RIGHT: *Many birds are much easier to see in spring while they are displaying. The Whitethroat literally throws itself into the air during its song flight!*

BELOW: *The Mistle Thrush is an easy species to track down in late winter and spring. It sings its wild, far-carrying song from the most exposed places.*

easily, although they tend to be concentrated in flocks. Many birds are so engrossed with feeding and maintaining their vital fat levels that they allow a closer approach than usual in winter. Conserving energy is also vital, so they are reluctant to take flight or move elsewhere unless they really have to, providing you with superb views to help you beat the winter chill.

SPRING

On display

Many birds become much more obvious in spring as they start to display in preparation for the breeding season. The sense of excitement and urgency is tangible, and it is a soul-lifting experience to be out at this time as the days begin to lengthen and the weather improves.

The marvel of bird song is the centrepiece of display for most birds. Resident songsters start to tune up from late winter, and throughout the spring, they are joined by more and more migrants from Africa. By May, the variety of song is astounding. This is the month for getting up early and enjoying the full intensity of the dawn chorus: an awe-inspiring experience that you should make the effort to enjoy at least once every year.

Since birds are singing a lot, they advertise themselves to people as well as other birds. It is possible to stand in one spot and make a mental map of what birds are present around you, so you know what is about and where to head to track down each songster.

The spring is a particularly good time for looking for tricky species that you may struggle to see at other times of the year. I always search for elusive woodland species such as Lesser Spotted Woodpecker and Hawfinch in March when they are at their most obvious and before there are too many leaves on the trees, and Goshawk when they are at their easiest to see as they display high over their woodland nesting sites. In fact, many birds perform elaborate displays, which are not only entertaining to watch, but are designed to make themselves as visible as possible to potential mates and rivals. They can become so engrossed in their songs and displays that they may even forget you are there.

top tip

Singing birds usually stick to a small area – their territory – and do not move about as much as at other times of year. They may even use exactly the same 'songpost', which makes it easier to find them.

BELOW: *Springtime is a fantastic time to be out watching birds as the countryside bursts into colour.*

ABOVE: *Even common birds are well worth a closer look in spring. Adult Grey Herons (foreground) look particularly handsome when they come into 'breeding condition'.*

Coming into colour

Many birds are at their best in terms of appearance at the start of the nesting season, so if you want pristine plumage, bright colours and impressive appendages, spring is the time to look.

Adult birds look fresh and neat as they come into breeding condition. Little Egrets gain their ornate plumes, or 'aigrettes', and look particularly handsome; Puffins develop their multicoloured bills; and Black-headed Gulls acquire their

distinctive chocolate-brown 'hoods'. You may also be lucky enough to witness lingering winter visitors such as Brambling and Water Pipit in their breeding finery.

Ruff, in all fairness, are quite often a disappointment. They are probably depicted as being one of the most eye-popping birds in your field guide, but the males possess their amazing breeding dress for only a few weeks each year. It is usually May before the males come into full colour, ready to joust in communal leks for the attentions of females.

Spring passage

The first major movement of birds of the year is the so-called spring passage – the arrival of birds such as Swallow, Turtle Dove and Whitethroat that spend the winter in Africa and fly north to Europe to take advantage of abundant nest sites and food supplies. Some individuals will nest here, while others merely pass through, stopping to feed up and rest at suitable 'stop overs' en route. At the same time, numbers of wintering birds decline sharply as they depart northwards for their breeding grounds, adding to the procession of birds.

BELOW: *Migrants, such as this male Redstart, can turn up anywhere in spring and autumn, well away from their usual breeding grounds.*

Spring migration can be rather hit and miss. There can be days when there are very few migrants to see because they may have moved through quickly or simply have not arrived yet. There will also be days when you just don't know where to look next as migrant birds pour in. The weather has a major part to play (see pages 106–8).

Migrant birds are in a hurry in spring. The race is on to get to the breeding grounds first, claim the best territories, and attract a mate. Consequently, many spring migrants do not hang around for long. Some may only be present for a matter of hours, before continuing on their journey – but this adds to the excitement. If you are planning to go and 'twitch' a bird in the spring, it is usually a good idea to move quickly.

The first sighting of a migrant marks spring proper for the birdwatcher. Garganey, Little Ringed Plover, Chiffchaff, Wheatear and Sand Martin are usually the first to arrive in March. In some years, spring migration can be very slow to get going and it can be mid-April before you begin to see trans-African migrants on a regular basis. Different species also have different windows of passage. Sand Martin passage may be almost over by the time Spotted Flycatchers begin to arrive in mid-May.

Large numbers of Arctic-bound waders, all in their breeding finery, pass through in spring. You may be lucky enough to stumble upon a trip of Dotterel in a field, find a Temminck's Stint at your local gravel pits, or see glamour birds such as Spotted Redshanks in their breeding dress. Many usually coastal waders also make

short-cuts across country and can be found pausing on the margins of gravel pits or your local sewage works. Tired waders may drop in at even the smallest wetlands to rest and refuel for a short period, before continuing their northward journey.

Spring is the season for looking for unusual birds that have overshot their breeding grounds in Southern Europe. Exciting birds such as Black Kite, Hoopoe, Great Spotted Cuckoo and Bee-eater regularly arrive in small numbers in North-west Europe at this time and you may just strike it lucky.

By the end of May, spring passage is all but over in most areas. Those migrants that remain will become temporary residents for a few months and stay and breed in the region.

OPPOSITE BOTTOM: *Seabird colonies are great locations for a good day's birding in summer. There will be masses of birds, which are guaranteed to show well and their behaviour is fascinating to watch.*

SUMMER

Spring migration has ground to a halt and the main 'return' passage seems like an age away, so what do you do to make the most of the quiet summer months and beat the birdwatcher's midsummer blues?

June, July and the first half of August are some of the quietest periods in the birding calendar. Many birders turn their attention to other more visible forms of wildlife at this time, such as butterflies or dragonflies, but there is no need to hang up your bins. You can enjoy good summer birding, although you do need to pick the right location and the right birds to look for, or at least lower your expectations of what you hope to see.

Most birds are busy nesting at this time and so can be very hard to see. If the females of a species are sitting on eggs, then your chances of a sighting are halved before you even start. After the youngsters have hatched, however, parent birds become easier to see again. Feeding a nest full of hungry mouths is a full-time job. Parents have to make several visits to the nest each day (hundreds in the case of Blue Tits) so if you know the whereabouts of a nest, you can simply wait for the parents to arrive or make a

RIGHT: *Summer is a great time to observe and enjoy bird behaviour. This Wren has its hands full with a fast-growing and hungry brood of youngsters.*

flypast on their regular route to and from the nest. Once the young have left the nest, your chances of a sighting can be seriously improved by the extra birds.

Summer also has its advantages when it comes to birding time. There are plenty of daylight hours to play with so you have the luxury of being able to spend long periods at a site. This gives you time to really cover sites properly and ensures you don't overlook birds because you are in a hurry to dash off. You can also take in many sites and even fulfil other obligations between birding sessions!

ABOVE: *You may be lucky enough to stumble across young Tawny Owls in summer.*

AUTUMN

Autumn is the most exciting season in the birding calendar. It is *the* season of migration and a huge number and variety of birds are on the move virtually everywhere. The period from late

August into early November represents one of the best of the year and you should aim to get into the field as often as possible.

Autumn passage is perhaps best referred to as 'return' passage because it commences as early as late June when waders that have failed to breed successfully, often including species such as Green Sandpiper, make an appearance. The bulk of migrants in the autumn are birds that have bred outside the region (usually further north and east) passing through on their way to Africa, although seabirds that have bred as far away as the Southern Oceans also pass through European waters.

A major plus point with return passage is that birds generally stay for longer than during the more rushed spring passage – sometimes weeks as opposed to days or even hours. The pressure is off as the main objective of reproduction has

been achieved or at least attempted. Birds are in no hurry to get to their wintering grounds and they take the opportunity to have a good rest and refuel. There are many more migrants in the autumn too as there are juvenile birds in abundance.

Birds seem to be on the move everywhere you look or go in autumn. The coast is a particularly exciting place to be as most migrants make first landfall there. It is the best seawatching season, too, and there is a chance to encounter birds such as shearwaters, skuas and petrels all around the coast (see pages 80–2).

The first waders to return during the second major wader passage of the year are adults. Juveniles come later and swell the numbers further. Flocks of Dunlin may contain Little Stint and Curlew Sandpiper or even something really special, such as a Pectoral Sandpiper. Rare and interesting birds can almost be expected in September and October, alongside the more regular passage migrants. Many become disorientated by bad weather or simply set off the wrong way from their breeding grounds – a phenomenon known as reverse migration. Inexperienced juvenile birds are particularly prone to becoming lost, brightening up many a birder's day in the process. The feeling that something special could be just around the corner or appear in the next bush is never far away in autumn.

Vagrants from Siberia and further east appear in late autumn and there are regular arrivals of exciting birds such as Richard's Pipit and Yellow-browed and Pallas's Warblers. American birds regularly appear in small numbers, too, especially in October. Finding or seeing a bird from so far away is for many one of the greatest thrills of birdwatching.

As resident birds begin to form post-breeding flocks, wintering birds start to arrive from the north. Large numbers of wildfowl can be seen arriving over the sea and immigrants such as thrushes, starlings and finches pour in. They cross over with the departing summer visitors to complete the birding calendar.

OPPOSITE TOP: *You never know what may appear next during autumn. Perhaps a tired, newly arrived Long-eared Owl will be roosting in the next tree.*

OPPOSITE BOTTOM: *The Barred Warbler is a scarce migrant from Eastern Europe that appears at coastal localities during autumn, often after easterly winds.*

BELOW: *The autumn berry crop is a welcome source of food for tired and hungry migrants. Wintering Redwings begin to arrive from Iceland and Scandinavia from mid-September.*

BELOW: *The coast is one of the most exciting places to go birding. You may have an entire beach full of birds to yourself in winter.*

Right place, wrong time

Many years ago, I asked my parents to take me to an oak woodland nature reserve in Staffordshire in August, excited by the promise of Redstart, Wood Warbler and Pied Flycatcher. I learned a harsh lesson that day about when to visit woodlands. By late summer, many birds have fallen silent and are remarkably unobtrusive in their behaviour. To say we did not see a single bird is hardly an exaggeration!

Lakes and reservoirs may be used for watersports during summer and coastal areas may be invaded by holidaymakers, so be warned if you are hoping for a quiet day's birding during the tourist season. Another thing to bear in mind is that some areas are quiet in winter when summer visiting migrants have departed, leaving only a handful of truly resident species. Heaths, moors and upland areas all fall into this category.

TIMES OF DAY

The early bird...

Whether you enjoy getting up with the lark or not (I know I am not quite so eager to be up at daybreak as I was in my younger days), there is no denying that the effort of getting up early will nearly always pay off. Bird activity is at a peak at this time and many birds are a lot easier to see at, or soon after, dawn.

Bird song is certainly at its most intense at this time of day, so you have to be up at the crack of dawn to appreciate the full effect of the dawn chorus. If you are planning to visit woodland, it is best to get there as early as possible as the birds will always be most active first thing.

Early starts are also a must at migration times. Many migrants arrive overnight and then move on soon after daybreak. Arriving on site at dawn during spring and autumn will produce more migrant birds. Seabird passage usually peaks in the first hour or two after dawn, as does 'visible migration' (see Chapter 4).

Winding down

The middle of the day is a notoriously quiet period for bird activity. In summer during the hottest part of the day, most birds are less active and busy trying to keep cool, so they can be much harder to find. Bird song and display virtually ceases and migration also slows considerably. Even though this 'hot

ABOVE: *The beautiful 'spinning coin' song of the Wood Warbler will lead you to many sightings of this attractive species.*

BELOW: *Many birds take to the skies to take advantage of rising thermals, even Carrion Crows.*

spot' won't have an effect in autumn and winter, you will still find that many birds are less active. In fact, the middle part of the day can be a good time to take a break.

Some birds, however, take full advantage of the heat, providing you with the best chance of seeing them. Rising pockets of warm air, or thermals, enable raptors to spend long periods in the air with the minimum of effort – especially convenient for displaying raptors. They simply spread their wings and tails and let the warm air do the hard work for them. When all goes quiet during hot days, a raptor watch is often a good choice.

Dusk

ABOVE: *The hottest part of the day is an excellent time to search for Golden Eagles.*

BELOW: *The sight of half a million Starlings swirling around above their roost is hard to beat for sheer 'wow' factor.*

One of my favourite times of day is the hour or so before darkness falls. It is a time of tremendous activity among birds as they head to their roosts and is also an excellent time for certain species that are otherwise difficult to see. Waiting for birds to come into roost is a great way of letting them come to you. Most birds will spend the night in exactly the same place and many roosts have been used for years, so you can almost be guaranteed of a sighting if you are prepared to linger. Too

many birders up sticks and head for home before the light begins to fade and miss out on some of the best birding of the day.

Many birds roost communally and provide spectacular scenes as they assemble or fly into their roosts in droves. Flights of wild geese and swans passing over to their roosts while calling evocatively are the perfect end to any winter's day. But it is not just the unusual birds that make the dusk period so enjoyable. All manner of passerines, from corvids (members of the crow family) to Pied Wagtails, roost in large numbers, and sometimes they provide an amazing spectacle. Even if you are not a fan of gulls, there is no denying their beauty when thousands fly over and settle on a lake like a carpet of snow (see pages 82–3).

Sightings of Hen Harrier and Merlin are hard to guarantee during the day as these species have such large hunting ranges. However, they both form communal roosts outside the breeding season, at which they assemble during the last hour or so of daylight. They often share roost sites as the former like to roost in reedbeds and tall vegetation; the latter perch on bushes. Many roosts are well known to birdwatchers. There may be one near you, or you could even try to discover one for yourself.

Owls come out to hunt at dusk, and this is also the time to search for Woodcock and – during summer – Nightjar. Species that aren't necessarily nocturnal or even crepuscular (active at dawn and dusk) often show better as the light begins to fade. Bittern and Water Rail both show a spurt of activity towards the end of the day. The latter emerge from cover with a little more confidence than usual to feed in the open, and the former may make flights to their roost sites in the reeds. Bitterns often roost in the same area and can appear at exactly the same time on winter afternoons.

Little Egrets can also provide some excellent end-of-day birding. They fly in from their daytime feeding grounds on estuaries and marshes to roost communally in large numbers, often perched up in trees and bushes, glowing like beacons in the half-light.

ABOVE: *Nightjars become active at dusk and provide a perfect end to a summer's day birding as they perform their bizarre displays and hunt for moths on heathland and in woodland clearings.*

TOP: *Watch for Woodcocks 'roding' over woods at dawn and dusk in spring and early summer. They patrol a regular beat as they display so you can enjoy excellent views without having to move from one spot.*

ABOVE: *Strong winds ensure that small birds, such as this Cetti's Warbler, keep well down in vegetation and usually out of sight.*

BELOW: *Autumn gales in October and November regularly 'blow' Grey Phalaropes onto the coast and even inland waters when they often provide outstanding views.*

THE WEATHER

The weather plays a big part in the way birds behave and therefore in which species you might see. Having a basic knowledge of the weather and the effect it has on birds is an invaluable piece of fieldcraft.

Still days are obviously the best for hearing birds and sunny days are pleasant, but remember that heat haze can become a problem if you are looking over long distances and that the sun may be in your eyes at times. Remember too that the sun rises in the east and sets in the west so that you can make sure you are standing in the right place at the right time.

It can be fun trying to guess what birds may appear or what effect the current conditions or certain events may have on birds. Some weather conditions can have dramatic effects on birds. The 'Great Storm' of October 1987 is legendary in birding circles for sweeping large numbers of rare seabirds such as Sabine's Gull and Grey Phalarope from the Bay of Biscay onto Britain's inland reservoirs.

Onshore gales should see seawatchers heading for the coast, while birders inland head for the local reservoir hoping for a storm-driven seabird. Sometimes the day after the 'big blow' is even better as the birds may still be there and conditions are less uncomfortable. Big freeze-ups can be bad news for birds, but

top tip

Get in the habit of watching the weather forecast before you go birdwatching and plan your trip accordingly. After all, you don't want your big day out spoiled by the thick fog that was forecast to linger all day or your special raptor-watching trip spoiled by heavy rain and strong winds.

good for birdwatchers. Hard weather further north and east can see birds migrating to milder climes and ice-free areas, resulting in large arrivals of wildfowl and other birds.

The weather plays a huge part in migration. Calm and clear weather encourages migration and enables birds to pass through quickly en route to their destination, but mist and drizzle can stop their progress altogether and force migrants to become 'grounded' until the weather improves. Poor weather can also disorientate birds and bring vagrants to unusual locations, much to the delight of birders. An airstream from a southerly quarter will encourage northward migration from Africa in spring, but northerly airflows at this time may bring migration to a halt. Birders hope for easterly winds in autumn to help 'drift' in birds from Eastern Europe and Siberia.

The weather will often dash your hopes of a good day's birding, but it can also produce the conditions that bring memorable birding experiences – and exciting birds.

ABOVE: *Easterly winds in spring and autumn divert migrating Black Terns across the North Sea to Britain where drizzle can force them to stop off at lakes and reservoirs to feed for a while.*

WHERE'S IT FROM?

ABOVE: *Water Rails can be very hard to see, but this all changes during winter freeze-ups when they emerge onto the ice in search of food.*

You will almost certainly find yourself asking the question: 'Where is this bird from?' every now and again. Having the ability to work out where the birds you see have come from, or at least to make an educated guess at their likely origin, is a useful skill. It will help you to think about and get to know birds and their movements and behaviour.

A bird's behaviour and age, when, where and in what habitat it has turned up, the prevailing weather conditions at the time, and the species with which it is associating can all help you to decide where a bird has come from and why.

Many individuals of species that you might think of as common residents will have come from much further away than you may realize. The coastal wood full of Robins one October day after a day of clear skies over Scandinavia and a light north-easterly breeze will consist of birds of Scandinavian origin, and the large groups of Starlings flying in high over your local hills in November may well be of Russian origin.

The question of 'origin' frequently arises when an unusual bird arrives and birdwatchers have to decide if it is a genuine wild vagrant or has escaped from the local cage and aviary bird show. When I first started birdwatching, one of my dream birds was the Red-breasted Goose. I actually found the first one I ever saw myself, on one of my local patches, so it should have been the perfect scenario, but in fact it was a huge disappointment. There was no doubt that it was a beautiful bird, but it had attached itself to the local flock of Canada Geese and was an obvious escapee. I had to wait a few years before I could add this species to my British list when I saw a first-winter bird among hundreds of dark-bellied Brent Geese – the favoured and most frequent 'carrier species' for genuine vagrants in the UK.

In the majority of cases, the origin of a bird will remain unknown for certain, but it is always interesting and educational to ask yourself where the birds you are watching may have come from and to speculate how they got there.

BELOW: *This dainty 'Richardson's' Canada Goose probably joined up with its Barnacle Geese hosts in Greenland and accompanied them to their wintering grounds in North-west Europe.*

6 PATCHWORK AND BIRD FINDING

There are no rules for how you should watch birds, but having an area you visit on a regular basis – a local patch – will open up a world of new birding excitement for you. I cannot recommend it enough. Here, you can become an expert on the birds of one area and can really think of them as your 'own'.

Local patches will also bring many exciting discoveries. One of the greatest pleasures of birdwatching is the thrill of discovering something new or unusual yourself. There is nothing wrong with being shown birds or with travelling to see a bird that has been found by someone else (like many 'twitchers') but your own discoveries will give you so much more pleasure.

A REGULAR BEAT

Every birder should have an area that they visit on a regular basis. 'Local patches' can be anywhere, be of any size and consist of any habitat. The choice is entirely yours. More often than not, they take the form of local gravel pits, sewage works, parks or reservoirs since most birders do not have the luxury of living within spitting distance of the best coastal marsh. Many local patches are adopted simply because they are near to home.

Once I had exhausted the potential of my local park, I took on a series of gravel pits near my home as a local patch. Water is a key element of a really good patch. As well as having an obvious attraction to water birds, stretches of water – especially rivers – also act as flyways for migrant birds and I was keen to make the most of my new discovery. I used to have a bike ride of 6.5 kilometres (4 miles) in total to reach my first patch that had water, usually before or after school, braving the hazards of traffic hurtling past at high speed, icy roads and the gale-force winds that can sweep across the Cambridgeshire Fens.

OPPOSITE: *Find yourself a local patch and visit it regularly – you won't regret it!*

BELOW: *Gravel pits make the perfect local patch. More are being created all the time so there could well be some near you ready to be adopted as your patch.*

ABOVE: *Dawn at Welches Dam on the Ouse Washes. Early starts often pay dividends for birders.*

BELOW: *Even relatively common birds such as Pintails take on a much greater significance if you see them on your patch.*

This may not paint a very pretty picture of my first patch-watching experiences, but those days actually provided me with some of my most enjoyable and rewarding birdwatching ever. It was truly addictive and I made the trip as often as I could. I can honestly say I was well rewarded by my efforts (well, most of the time!). Witnessing the variations in your local bird life is fascinating and the more you visit, the more you will see and learn. Local patch-watching enables you to see at first hand the daily variations that go on in an area; for example, the build-up of wintering Coot; the first Sedge Warbler of spring; and the ups and downs of the breeding birds, all of which will bring you enormous pleasure. There will be more quiet days than good ones, but these only make those days when you do see something interesting all the more enjoyable.

Birds can take on a whole new meaning if you see them on your patch. Some species will be rarities even if they are common birds elsewhere. You wouldn't be too surprised to see a Sanderling scurrying along the beach at the coast, but the one you find on the margins of your local reservoir will be a wholly more exciting experience. Local patches are also great places to learn about birds and to practise your identification skills and fieldcraft in a place you know well. You will soon discover which areas are good for which species, how the birds behave there, which species appear when and whether they do only under certain conditions.

It is interesting to see if events at your patch are a reflection of trends at a wider level and this will raise all sorts of fascinating questions. Is the shortage of Cuckoos a sign that they are rare this summer or because there are fewer nests of Reed Warblers in which to lay their eggs? Is the late arrival of Fieldfares or the larger than usual numbers of Goosanders apparent elsewhere?

Once you have a patch, try to visit frequently: certainly once a week, but more if you can. It is a shame to be beaten to finding a good bird by the birder who visited on the one day you decided to have an extra half an hour in bed. A friend of mine had been religiously watching his local gravel pits for about 20 years, but

BELOW: *Finding scarce migrants, such as this Wood Sandpiper, is one of the many thrills of local patchwork.*

one morning during an excellent September wader passage, he chose not to make a visit. Another friend found Britain's sixth Red-necked Stint there that morning and put the gravel pits firmly on the birding map. Needless to say, the first friend was kicking himself and probably will do until his dying day.

I have no doubt that the apprenticeship I served at my first local patch made me a better birder. Every other 'local patcher' you speak to will probably say the same.

FINDING YOUR OWN BIRDS

At some point or another, most birder's thoughts have turned to finding a rare bird. The excitement of finding my first – a juvenile Purple Heron that spent a month at my local gravel pits one autumn – took months to fade away.

Regularly working your local patch and concentrating your efforts on one area on a regular basis will seriously improve your chances of making a good find. A large number of unusual birds are actually found by hard-working 'local patchers'. They are the reward for the many hours' work you put in and for putting up with the quieter days. Even the most uninspiring patch has the potential to surprise, delight and produce the odd really exciting sighting. There are some wonderful and legendary birding tales of people finding birds in bizarre locations. A friend of mine once found a Rustic Bunting spending the winter

BELOW: *Gatherings of even the commonest birds can harbour exciting rarities. Careful scrutiny of your local Starling flocks could produce a Rose-coloured Starling: an irruptive immigrant from South-east Europe.*

among the Reed Buntings and Yellowhammers in a stubble field only a few kilometres from his home.

Even if your local patch is your back garden, regular watching will turn up surprises. Perhaps a Chiffchaff or a Blackcap will spend the winter or a Brambling may throw in its lot with your local Chaffinches. Many truly rare birds have been found in people's gardens over the years – even 'mega-rarities' from America. Garden watchers in England have recently found Ovenbird and Baltimore Oriole wintering in their gardens alongside their local Blackbirds, Robins and Blue Tits! Well, we can all dream…

I used to be driven by the thought of finding rare and unusual birds as a young birder, but living 64 kilometres (40 miles) from the coast, I realized the chances of finding a Siberian vagrant were very small. However, I did have around 30,000 Wigeon spending every winter just up the road on the Ouse Washes, so I devoted my time to scrutinizing the flocks for American Wigeon (and yes, it did work as I have found three so far).

ABOVE: *The handsome Great Grey Shrike is always an exciting find.*

Many of the most successful bird-finders go in search of particular rare species by looking in the right habitats at the right time of year in this way. Thinking about which species are likely to occur at certain times and whether certain weather conditions will influence their arrival will certainly improve the likelihood of you finding something unusual.

It sounds obvious, but always look at every bird you see, wherever you are, and carefully check every flock and large gathering of birds you find. Look out for the key conditions that aid migration and may assist the arrival of vagrants (see pages 106–7). And don't forget, the more you go out, the more chance you have of bumping into something unusual.

Influxes and arrivals

Some birds are sporadic in their appearances – rare in some years but widespread in others – so you may go long periods without seeing them. These are the charismatic species that are prone to periodic influxes.

During influx years, take the chance to enjoy the birds, as it could be some time before you see one (or certainly as many)

top tip

Keep your ear to the ground to see whether it is a 'good' year for a certain species or whether any large-scale arrivals have taken place, and use the information to your advantage to find your own birds.

ABOVE: *Small numbers of Pallas's Warblers arrive in North-west Europe during October and November. They inevitably arrive in 'waves' so if there is one, there will almost certainly be more, so why not go in search of your own?*

OPPOSITE BOTTOM: *Northerly gales in late autumn and winter can bring large numbers of Little Auks southwards into the North Sea, but in other years there may be hardly any!*

again. It is also a golden opportunity to find your own individuals of the species involved, perhaps even on your local patch. Of the rarer species, a spectacular invasion of Arctic Redpolls occurred in Britain in the winter of 1995–96, while Red-footed Falcons arrived en masse in the spring of 1992. Many birdwatchers seized the opportunity to get out and find their own on their local patch, and some of them proved lucky.

Natural effects are usually the cause of these influxes. The weather brought in the 'Red-foots', with a prolonged spell of winds from their breeding grounds in South-east Europe, while plummeting temperatures in the north brought in the Arctic Redpolls with masses of Mealy Redpolls. Food availability often triggers these events. The periodic large-scale autumn and winter arrivals of Rough-legged Buzzards are linked to the fluctuating cycle of their lemming and vole prey in Scandinavia and Arctic Russia. Waxwings arrive in Britain in large numbers only when the berry crop is poor or exhausted on the continent.

It is not just about rare birds, though. Wildfowl may arrive in large numbers in hard winters, certain waders or skuas may have a good breeding season (resulting in large numbers of autumn juveniles passing through), Crossbills occasionally 'invade' and become commoner following the failure of the coniferous forest cone crop elsewhere and Quails sometimes seem to call from every field in 'Quail summers'.

If you hear that a spectacular arrival of migrants has occurred on the coast, then why not try to experience the excitement at less well-watched locations, which will almost certainly have received a similar influx of birds? Even influxes that may seem far away can have far-reaching effects from

ABOVE: *The Red-spotted Bluethroat is a scarce migrant to Britain that can occur in large-scale influxes if the winds are from the East in May.*

which you may benefit. A massive 'fall' (landfall) of thousands of Redstarts occurred on England's east coast one September, and I was able to benefit from the event and enjoy the rare sight of this species at my local gravel pits, miles inland, as the birds filtered across the country.

BIRDING ETIQUETTE

Birding has become an increasingly popular and sociable hobby and you will almost certainly find yourself meeting other birders when out in the field. Uttering the time-honoured phrases, 'Seen much?' or 'Anything about?', is the perfect way of entering into conversation with fellow birders. It can be a very useful piece of 'fieldcraft' and will certainly help you to see birds!

I have always enjoyed talking to other birdwatchers I meet. Most birdwatchers love talking about birds as much as watching them! It is nice to share sightings and you will often find they have a nugget of useful information for you in exchange for your sightings. I have made many friends in this way and have learned – and still learn – an awful lot from the people that I chat to. Visiting a new area can be rather daunting, but you will find that most locals are more than pleased to point you in the direction of the best spots and to tell you what birds have been seen recently.

BELOW: *Birdwatching continues to grow in popularity all the time. You can always while away the quieter moments by chatting to fellow birders.*

top tip

The internet is a fantastic source of information for every aspect of birds and birding. There are hundreds of websites devoted to everything from top birding spots and rare bird sighting information to discussion groups and bird clubs.

Twitching

Most birdwatchers are not twitchers at all, contrary to what the popular press says! In fact, many birders hate being labelled with the tag of 'twitcher'. Real twitchers have a passion for seeing the rarest species and for building up as big a list of different species as possible. Most of the birds they go to see will have been found by someone else and they find out about them from the bird information 'grapevine', which alerts them (nowadays often via pagers) to the whereabouts of rare birds.

I bet there are very few birders who haven't 'twitched' a bird at some time. Who wouldn't walk a hundred metres down a path to see a Wryneck that the birder you have just met saw half an hour earlier? This is exactly the same principle as twitching birds over longer distances. If you get the chance to see a rare bird, my advice would be to do it. It can be immensely exciting and you may well never see another in your lifetime. Seeing unusual birds is also very educational from an identification point of view. There is nothing wrong with going to see other people's birds – I know I love to share my finds with others – so treat yourself from time to time and enjoy the experience.

ABOVE: *The Siberian Rubythroat – particularly the male – is a dream bird for birdwatchers in North-west Europe and one that few would waste any time in going to twitch!*

ABOVE: *The arrival of a rare bird will generate a huge amount of interest. The crowd here has gathered to catch a glimpse of a Swainson's Thrush from America.*

I do a fair amount of 'twitching' and get a great deal of pleasure out of every rare and unusual bird I see, but I also put in many hours at my local patches and find a fair few good birds each year. My advice would be to mix your birding up and enjoy as many different experiences as you can.

Twitching is not for everyone, though. I remember getting far more excited about the group of Bearded Tits I found in a ditch than the Oriental Pratincole I had gone to see on my first ever twitch!

KEEPING A RECORD

I have kept a diary of my birdwatching activities ever since my first foray into the field. This huge volume of information is one of my most treasured possessions and is the thing I would most want to save from a fire in my house! It is great to reminisce on past adventures and 'glory days', but keeping a record of your sightings also has a more practical value.

I often look back to previous year's diaries to see what I did on a certain date and to remind myself of what I saw. Your past records can be a great way of helping you plan future days in the field. If you had good views of your local pair of Long-eared Owls on a certain date, or found Whinchat regularly in a certain place for a couple of weeks, then you can repeat the process again another year and hopefully get a similar result. If you enjoyed a particularly good seawatch or the arrival of migrants on a certain day, you can see what weather conditions there were at the time and look for them again.

A FINAL THOUGHT

After reading this book, I hope you are filled with new enthusiasm, and hopefully some new knowledge, and are inspired to try out at least some of the tips and techniques that have been described. Don't forget the more birds you see and the more time you spend in the field, the better your identification and fieldcraft skills will become. So there you have it: the perfect excuse to go birdwatching! Finally, I would like to wish you good luck in your birdwatching adventures and hope you enjoy the greatest of success.

ABOVE: *Keeping a record of your sightings will allow you to try and beat previous years' 'earliest' and 'latest' dates for sightings of migrants such as the Swallow.*

LEFT: *Your field notebooks will become a priceless permanent record of your birding experiences. You can record as many or as few details as you like, but don't forget to submit your records to your county recorder.*

USEFUL ADDRESSES

Birdlife International
Wellbrook Court
Girton Road
Cambridge CB3 0NA
Tel: 01223 277 318
birdlife@birdlife.org
www.birdlife.net

British Birdwatching Fair
British Birdwatching Fair Office
Fishponds Cottage
Hambleton Road
Oakham
Rutland LE15 8AB
Tel: 01572 771 079
enquiries@birdfair.org.uk
www.birdfair.org.uk

BTO (British Trust for Ornithology)
The Nunnery
Thetford
Norfolk IP24 2PU
Tel: 01842 750 050
info@bto.org
www.bto.org

RSPB (Royal Society for the Protection
of Birds)
The Lodge
Sandy
Bedfordshire SG19 2DL
Tel: 01767 680 551
info@rspb.org.uk
www.rspb.org

The Wildlife Trusts
The Kiln
Waterside
Mather Road,
Newark

Nottinghamshire NG24 1WT
Tel: 0870 036 7711
info@wildlife-trusts.cix.co.uk
www.wildlifetrusts.org

WWT (The Wildfowl & Wetlands Trust)
Slimbridge
Gloucestershire GL2 7BT
Tel: 01453 891 900
enquiries@wwt.org.uk
www.wwt.org.uk

Recommended Birding Websites

www.surfbirds.com
www.birdforum.net
www.fatbirder.com
www.birdguides.com

FURTHER READING

Books

Bill Oddie's Birds of Britain and Ireland
(New Holland, 1998)

Bill Oddie's Introduction to Birdwatching
(New Holland, 2002)

Birds by Behaviour
Dominic Couzens (HaperCollins, 2003)

Birds of Europe
Lars Jonsson (A&C Black, 1996)

Birdwatcher's Pocket Field Guide
Mark Golley (New Holland, 2003)

Collins Bird Guide
Lars Svensson, Peter Grant, Killian
Mullarney & Dan Zetterström
(HaperCollins, 2001)

*Handbook of Bird Identification for Europe
and the Western Palearctic*
Mark Beaman and Steve Madge
(Helm, 1998)

How to Birdwatch
Stephen Moss (New Holland, 2003)

*Pocket Guide to the Birds of Britain and
North-West Europe*
Chris Kightley, Steve Madge and Dave
Nurney (Pica Press, 1998)

RSPB Handbook of British Birds
Peter Holden and Tim Cleeves
(Helm, 2002)

Understanding Bird Behaviour
Stephen Moss (New Holland, 2003)

Where to Watch Birds in Britain and Ireland
David Tipling (New Holland, 2004)

Magazines and Journals

Bird Watching
Available monthly from newsagents or by
subscription from
Emap Active Ltd
Bretton Court
Bretton
Peterborough PE3 8DZ
Tel: 0845 601 1356
emap@subscription.co.uk

Birding World
Available by subscription from
Stonerunner
Coast Road
Cley next the Sea
Holt
Norfolk NR25 7RZ
Tel: 01263 741 139
sales@birdingworld.co.uk
www.birdingworld.freeserve.co.uk

Birdwatch
Available monthly from newsagents or by
subscription from
Warners
West Street
Bourne
Lincolnshire PE10 9PH
Tel: 01778 392 027
subscriptions@birdwatch.co.uk
www.birdwatch.co.uk

British Birds
Available by subscription from
The Banks
Mountfield
Robertsbridge
East Sussex TN32 5JY
Tel: 01580 882 039
subscriptions@britishbirds.co.uk
www.britishbirds.co.uk

Dutch Birding
Available by subscription from
Dutch Birding Association
c/o Jeannette Admiraal
Iepenlaan 11
1901 ST Castricum
Netherlands.
circulation@dutchbirding.nl
www.dutchbirding.nl

Alula
Available by subscription from
Alula Oy
Eestinkalliontie 16 D
FIN-02280 Espoo
Finland
antero.topp@alula.fi
www.alula.fi

The Birdwatcher's Yearbook
Published annually by
Buckingham Press
55 Thorpe Park Road
Peterborough PE3 6LJ
Tel: 01733 561 739
buck.press@btinternet.com

INDEX

AUTHOR'S ACKNOWLEDGEMENTS

I would like to thank the many people who have provided me with encouragement and inspiration during my first 14 years as a birdwatcher. In particular, I would like to thank my parents, who have given me tremendous support and who put themselves out on many occasions to take me birdwatching when I was a fanatically keen young birder.

I would also like to thank the many people I have met who share my passion for birds and with whom I have enjoyed countless magical moments in the field. I am fortunate enough now to be able to list lots of these people among my closest friends. There are too many to mention here, but I would especially like to thank Ade Cooper, Alan Hitchings, Colin Kirtland and Terry Murfitt.

I'd also like to thank Jo Hemmings and Camilla MacWhannell at New Holland, and the artists and photographers who provided the superb illustrations and photographs for this book.

Last but not least, I would like to thank the birds themselves for bringing me immeasurable pleasure in so many ways and for giving me an interest that has now become a way of life. Long may it continue.

PHOTOGRAPHS

All photographs by David Tipling except for the following:

David Cottridge: p22, p64, p65, p66, p83, p111, p118
Chris Gomersall: p78
Bob Glover/rspb-images.com: p83

ARTWORKS

All artworks by David Daly except for the following:

Clive Byers: p26 (t), p56 (b)
John Cox: p67, p77, p79, p85
Martin Elliott: p1 & 44 (t), p5 & 37 (t), p38 (b), p41 (b), p42, p43 (t), p45 (t), p47, p69, p86, p97 (t), p108
Stephen Message: p22, p34 (t), p35 (t), p37 (b), p40 (btl, bbl, bbr), p48 (t), p58 (t), p96 (t)